Once upon a time, Tesco was a global retail giant.

It was second most profitable retailer in the world and the fourth most profitable business in the UK.

At one point, for every twelve pounds spent in the UK, one pound went to Tesco.

Currently, Tesco is struggling to make a profit and its Chief Executive Officer Philip Clarke pins the blame on:

- The economic conditions
- The competition
- The internet

Meanwhile, while Mr. Clarke views the internet as an obstacle to Tesco profit, Next and Boots used the internet to boost their profit.

Richer Sound has maintained its rankings in the Guinness Book of Records for the highest sales per sq. ft. of any other retailer in the world.

Holland & Barrett remains the second most profitable business in the UK and Harrods continues to be the favourite shopping place for the rich and famous.

What is Tesco and other struggling retailers getting wrong that Harrods, Richer Sound, Next and Holland & Barrett are getting right?

What lessons can the rest of the retail industry learn from the success of Harrods, Richer Sound, Next and Boots?

How can other retailers replicate the success of Harrods, Richer Sound, Next and Boots?

The answer to these questions are in the 'How to Increase Retail Sales' workbook.

This workbook contains the latest innovative strategies for increasing retail sales and profit.

It contains the fundamental principles used by the most successful retailers that has been responsible for their success.

It is made up of four modules:

Module One: The psychology of store design and visual merchandising display.

Module Two: Store design blueprint: designing a functional retail store.

Module Three: How to create an attractive visual merchandising display.

Module Four: How to increase retail profit with effective loss prevention strategies.

Retail success is a formula.

How to Increase Retail Sales Workbook contains that formula.

***This book is the script of the presentation of the seven videos of the "How to Increase Retail Sales" home study course along with exercises to help you put into practice what you will learn.

Therefore, if you do not feel like reading the notes, you can go directly to the exercises.

> You can also acquire the home study course containing the video and audio if you prefer to watch or listen to the workshop.

About the Author

Romeo Richards is the founder of the Business Education Centre, an institution that shows professional entrepreneurs such as doctors, lawyers, dentists, consultants, trainers, coaches, retailers and security firm owners how to attract customers and grow their businesses.

He has authored twelve books on how to increase retails sales and profit. He is also the author of the "How to effectively market and manage a professional firm" series for doctors, lawyers, dentists, consultants, trainers, coaches and security firms.

He is the creator of:

- How to Increase Retail Sales' home study course
- How to Attract & Retain Customers' home study course
- The Law Firm Business Growth Blueprint: Three Step Formula For Growing A Law Firm' home study course
- The Accounting Firm Business Growth Blueprint: Three Step Formula For Growing An Accounting Firm' home study course
- The Private Medical Practice Business Growth Blueprint: Three Step Formula For Growing A Private Medical Practice' home study course
- The Dental Practice Business Growth Blueprint: Three Step Formula For Growing A Dental Practice' home study course
- The Business Growth Blueprint: Three Step Formula For Growing Any Business' home study course

- The Restaurant Business Growth Blueprint: Three Step Formula For Growing A Restaurant Business' home study course

He has authored several White Papers and regularly writes articles on marketing, business development and retail profit improvement.

Romeo is a captivating speaker and a business growth and marketing consultant.

You can reach Romeo by emailing:
romeo@theprofitexperts.co.uk
or call +44 (0)20 8798 0579

The workbook is a component of the 'How to Increase Retail Sales' home study course. The home study course contains seven DVDs, seven audio CDs and a workbook.

Purchase of the home study course comes with Skype and on site consultation and an invitation to exclusive private seminar taught by Romeo and other retail experts.

How to Increase Retail Sales

Workbook

Romeo Richards

www.romeorichards.com
+44 (0)20 8798 0579
romeo@theprofitexperts.co.uk

Copyright © 2014 The Business Education Center
Print Edition

Dedication

I wrote about vision as your reason for doing anything. I do what I do first and foremost to be an example to my son.

Secondly, to have the ability to help my people shed the curse of poverty.

Alex this book is for you!

Africa this book is in your honour!

Acknowledgements

My sincere gratitude to Mr. White for editing the book and Paul of BB eBooks for formatting it.

How to Increase Retail Sales

Workbook

Romeo Richards

www.romeorichards.com
+44 (0)20 8798 0579
romeo@theprofitexperts.co.uk

Table of Contents

About the Author	iii
Dedication	ix
Acknowledgements	xi
Why you should read this workbook	xix
Introduction	1

Module One: How to Influence Shoppers Behaviour with Store Design and Visual Merchandising Display — 5

Designing Your Store for Functionality	23
Workshop	29
How Do You Select Your Target Audience: Who Are You Going To Sell To?	32
Workshop	36
Crafting Your Marketing Message: What Are You Going to Sell to Them	38
Workshop	70
Your Marketing Media: How Are You Going to Sell to Them?	73
Your Website	95
Social Media	112
Workshop	115

Module Two: Store Design Blueprint: How to Use Store Design to Increase Sales — 119

Store Design for Functionality	120
How to Choose Your Store Colour and Layout	133
The Best Retail Store Lighting System	137

How To Choose The Right Materials For Store Design	150
Workshop	153

Module Three: Visual Merchandising Display — 157

How To Use Visual Merchandising to Increase Sales	157
How to Burst the Price Myth with Creative Merchandise Display	168
How to Maximise Display Space Allocation with Creative Display	180
The Benefits Planogram Software	187
Workshop	194

Module Four: How to Increase Retail Profit with Effective Loss Prevention Strategies — 199

Lessons from My Tesco Experience	203
How to Create a Culture of Loss Prevention	207
• What is retail shrinkage?	207
• How do you create a culture of loss prevention?	209
Workshop	217
How to Prevent Employee Theft	219
• So Why do Retail Employees Steal?	220
• How Does Employee Theft Take Place in a Retail Store?	220
• What are the Tell tail Signs of Employee Theft?	222
• How to Prevent Employee Theft	231
Workshop	236
How to Prevent Retail Employee Error	238
• What Is Retail Employee Error?	240
• Types of Employee Error	241
• How to Reduce Employee Error	260
Workshop	261
How to Create An Efficient Receiving Process	263

• The Supply Chain Dilemma	265
• How to Train Receiving Employees	267
• How to Prevent Receiving Losses	267
Workshop	268
Perishable and Non-Perishable Shrinkage	270
• Causes of Perishable Shrinkage	271
• How to Prevent Perishable Shrinkage	272
Workshop	273
Non-Perishable Shrinkage	275
• Classification of Non-Perishable Shrinkage	275
• Strategies for Preventing Non-Perishable Shrinkage	276
Workshop	278
How to Prevent Shoplifting	280
• Why Does Shoplifting Take Place?	281
• Organised Retail Crime (ORC): The New Dynamic in	
• Shoplifting	281
• Shoplifting Techniques	285
• Tell-Tale Signs of a Shoplifter	286
• How to Prevent Shoplifting	286
Workshop	288
Summary	290
Great Books by Romeo	295
Book Romeo	306

Why you should read this workbook

The aim of this workbook is to share with you fundamental principles and strategies for:

- Attracting customers to your store
- Retaining them for long in your store
- Persuading them to buy
- Triggering repeat visit (reduce refund)

The reason the workbook focuses on these four is this:

One

In order to increase sales, you first need to attract shoppers to your store.

Two

When they are inside the store, you need a mechanism for retaining them for long periods. Various studies reveal that the longer shoppers stay in a retail store, the higher the possibility of them buying.

Three

The fact that they stay long in your store does not necessarily mean they are automatically going to buy.

The majority of retailers underestimate the difficulties of getting people to part with their money.

Most of the time people agree with everything you say until it reaches the point of removing their wallets and paying for what you are offering them.

It is at this point that the large majority of sales break down.

So in a way, this point is the most important element of the four.

If you get this part right, you will be laughing your way to the bank.

You get it wrong and you might have to place one of those dreaded signs that reads "Closing Down Sale," at your storefront.

Unfortunately, this is the part where many retailers drop the ball.

They drive traffic into their store…retain them for long but then when it comes to the point of persuading them to buy they fall short.

Part two of the conversion process is up selling them…

When you have customers in your store, you might have spent a fortune to attract them. Now you want to extract the maximum amount of money from them.

Many people might feel uncomfortable with the phrase 'extracting the maximum amount of money' from their customers.

I am not suggesting you pressure them into buying or that you sell them things they do not want. I am suggesting you make them aware of offers in your store.

Therefore, it is important that you have a sales trigger that activates when someone buys an item. Everything in your store needs to be like a chain, a domino effect…one thing sets off the trigger; another thing sets off another trigger for something else, and so on.

Example: When someone buys a suit, it automatically triggers a shirt…tie…socks…shoe…etc.

Again, I must repeat this point. I am not suggesting you or your store assistants behave like obnoxious sales people who pressure shoppers into buying something they do not want. I am saying you offer them the opportunity to buy your other products.

There is a safe process for doing this. We will explore that safe process in the workbook.

Research shows that 20% of people will accept upsell during a transaction if it is offered to them.

Think what a difference an additional 20% increase in sales will have on your profit margin.

Four

The fourth point in the process is – How do you automatically trigger repeat purchase after the initial sales?

There are three ways to grow any business:

- Attract customers
- Increase the frequency of purchase
- Increase the value of purchase

Many retailers focus on the initial sales and forget about repeat sales.

Everyone who enters your store needs to be automatically considered a customer for life.

The moment they enter your store, your goal needs to be first, to move them from window shoppers to customers, then from customers to customers for life.

This is a very important process because by having that mind-set and instilling that into your store assistants, you drastically reduce refunds.

Furthermore, the service the person receives is completely different because in your mind you already know you want this person to return.

This brings us to probably the most important word of this entire workbook: *experience*.

As we move along in the workbook, I will expand on this point but I think it will be appropriate that I address it here briefly.

In many cities around the UK, the High Street is literally becoming a ghost town as one independent retailer after the other goes out of business.

At one point, the situation got so bad that the government was forced to intervene.

The government sat up the Mary Portas commission that spend millions of pounds to come up with recommendations that did not even scratch the surface of the root cause of the problem.

The reason these retailers go out of business is they failed to adapt to the *new retail environment*.

Those retailers want to run a 21st century retail operation with 19th century skill set.

The retail industry is changing rapidly.

Online shopping and the internet as a whole has completely changed consumers buying behaviour.

According to the centre for retail research, online shopping will reach two hundred and *twelve billion dollars* in Europe in 2014 *and three hundred and six billion dollars* in the US, in the same year.

Besides the fact that brick and mortar retailers are losing out to online shopping, the internet is placing tremendous pressure on brick and mortar retail profitability. Now retailers are forced to lower prices to compete with online retailers such as Amazon and eBay.

Amazon and eBay have destroyed certain retail categories.

Books and entertainment retailers are all but disappeared from the retail landscape.

Those still holding on are hanging by their teeth.

In the UK, the three largest books and entertainment retailers are on life support.

WH Smith sells more groceries than it does books.

Waterstones in on the brink, HMV is in administration (retail talk for about to go out of business). Well, actually it has already gone out of business; it is just buying time before it finally shuts its doors.

The reason these retailers are in trouble is they have not adjusted their strategies to take into account the *new retail environment*.

The retail industry has changed forever and it will continue to change.

It will never be the same again.

Those retailers who understand the current reality and adjust their operations to take into account the new dynamic are the ones who will survive or even prevail in the *new retail environment.*

Consumer buying behaviour has changed.

The consumer of today visits a retail store for a completely different reason from the consumer of five or ten years ago.

I am going to tell you one truth, the first amongst many other truths I will be telling you throughout this workbook.

That truth is this: No one comes to your store to buy your crappy made in China merchandise.

If you think in that manner and continue to think in that manner, you are living in another retail century.

In this *new retail environment,* people come to your store to buy an *experience…*

- The experience of your store design
- The experience of your visual merchandising display
- The experience of your customer service

Richer sound has the highest sales per sq. ft. than any other retailer in the entire world.

They have held that position for over twenty years.

In the same token, Richer Sound continues to win the 'Which' consumer survey for the most knowledgeable staff year after year.

Do you see the correlation between Richer Sound's knowledgeable staff and their profitability?

If you don't let me explain:

Richer Sound sells entertainment.

What's the problem most people face when making decision on entertainment or electronic products?

Confusion

Except tech savvy folks, the majority of ordinary people struggle to decide on the types of entertainment that is suitable for them.

Richer Sound management, aware of this fact ensure they train their staff up to a level at which they are capable of answering customers questions.

Remember their customers could buy the same stuff online for one tenth of the price they pay at Richer Sound.

Yet Richer Sound customers flood there to pay three times the price they could pay online.

Why?

Customers are not paying for the entertainment; they are paying for the service…*in order words they are paying for the experience.*

This is what the *new retail environment* is about.

How to create the Richer Sound experience in your store for your customers is what I am going to be sharing with you in this workbook.

Introduction

Increasing retail sales and profit requires:

- A good store design
- An attractive visual merchandising display
- An effective loss prevention strategy

When many retailers think about designing their stores, the first thing they do is, they put it out tender for shop fitters to bid for the contract and they choose the cheapest.

What they fail to realise is good store design is not about the shelves and fixtures; a good store design is about the aesthetics and ambiance.

Creating a good store design and an attractive visual merchandise display that attracts customers to your store must start with you answering the following three questions:

- Who are we trying to attract?
- What are we going to sell to them?
- How are we going to sell it to them?

These questions and answers form the core of module one of the "How to Increase Retail Sales" home study course workbook.

Module one addresses the psychology of store design and visual merchandising display.

In this module, you will learn:

- How to identify your target market: Who you are going to sell to
- How to craft a compelling marketing message: What you are going to sell to them
- How to select the right media for your marketing message: How you are going to sell it to them.

You will also learn:

- Lead generation: How to get customers to respond to your offers
- Lead conversion: How to get customers to buy when they are in store
- Customer retention: How to keep them as customers for life
- How to reduce missed opportunities in your store

Module two deals with:

- Designing Your Store For Functionality
- How To Increase Retail Sales With Attractive Store Designs
- Designing a Store For Increase Customer Flow
- How To Choose Your Store Colour and Layout
- The Best Retail Store Lighting System
- How To Wow Customers With Creative Storefront Designs
- How To Choose The Right Materials For Store Designs

Module three addresses:

- Creating an attractive visual merchandising display

You will learn:

- How to Use Visual Merchandising to Increase Sales
- Challenges Facing Visual Merchandisers
- How to Burst The Price Myth with Creative Merchandise Displays
- The Best Merchandise Display Strategy
- How To Maximise Display Space Allocation With Creative Displays
- The Benefits Planogram Software

Module four discusses increasing profit by reducing your shrinkage levels.

You will learn:

- How to Create a Culture of Loss Prevention
- How to Prevent Employee Theft
- How to Prevent Employee Error
- How to Create an Efficient Receiving Process
- How to Prevent Perishable Shrinkage
- How to Prevent Non-Perishable Shrinkage
- How to Prevent Shoplifting

In the How to Increase Retail Sales workbook, you will learn how to design your store well and create an attractive visual merchandising display so you can increase your sales and profit.

You will learn how to identify:

- Who you are going to sell to
- What you are going to sell to them
- How you are going to sell it to them

You will also learn how to increase your store's profit. (*To increase sales without simultaneously increasing profit is false economy.*)

Module One:

How to Influence Shoppers Behaviour with Store Design and Visual Merchandising Display

As I was writing this workbook, it was revealed that NEXT the second largest clothing retailer in the UK profit surpassed Marks & Spence's for the first time in its 32 years history.

The two main reasons given for the Next success were.

1. NEXT Home Directory has grown to become the UK's biggest home shopping business.
2. NEXT shifted its business model and adapted quickly to the online shopping behaviour of its customers.

A fashion retail consultant summarised NEXT success in a BBC interview better than NEXT CEO could have done.

She said '**NEXT understands its customers better than any other retailer.**'

That statement is huge as it validates the points I am going to be stressing and hammering throughout this workbook.

That point is '*know thy customers*'.

This is the foundation of store design and visual merchandise display.

I have a friend who recently graduated as an architect in Bulgaria.

He usually sends his drawing for me to see.

What I noticed is, whenever, he completed the drawing of a building, the drawing usually shows the building as it will look when it is occupied.

The car park will have cars parked in the parking bays, the offices will have people seated at desks as if working etc.

If it were a residential property, he would have people in the living and dining rooms; there will be someone in the washer and people lying on the bed in the rooms.

When I asked him why he created his designs in this manner, he said it was about '*functionality.*'

He said the building had to be designed to function the way people wanted it, not the other way around.

The occupants of a building are not supposed to adapt to a building instead it is the building that is supposed to adapt to the occupants.

I thought the concept was brilliant.

Let's now try to adapt this concept to designing your store.

What are the objectives of a store design?

- Attract customer to your store
- Retain them for long in your store
- Persuade them to buy

There might be other benefits of designing a beautiful store, for now let us stick to these three.

What is the first step in the process of attracting customers to a retail store?

The first step in the process is to know who you want to attract to your store.

Hence the reason I used the NEXT example.

If you know who you want to attract into your store, you will design your store to appeal to those customers.

This is where most independent and small retailers drop the ball.

You open your store, stock it with goods and hope the customers will show up to buy, simply because you are open for business.

That would have been possible once upon a time in a small village in Wales.

Ten twenty years ago many Asian entrepreneurs stuck gold when they opened newsagents in remote villages all around the UK.

At the time, they had no competition.

Then one morning the three hundred pounds gorillas by the name of Tesco and ASDA began encroaching on their territories.

By the time, they realised what hit them it was too late.

All but a handful of them went out of business.

The days when you just open a store and hope that someone will show up are gone.

Furthermore, to attempt such a practice on a High Street in the middle of London or Manchester is suicidal.

What do I mean by 'know thy customer'?

I am not suggesting you hire a research firm that asks shoppers a few insignificant questions that provide you with some insignificant data at the end of the process.

I mean standing at the entrance of your store yourself asking your customers what they think about your store as they walk in and out.

Gaining first-hand information from your customers, analysing that information and making merchandising and store design decisions based upon feedback from your customers.

This is the easiest and best way of knowing your customers.

This was the strategy used by Sam Walton that transformed Walt-Mart (ASDA) from a dime store to the biggest retailer in the world.

Many of the more successful retailers today are those founded upon the principle of, knowing thy customer.

Today as those retail organisations grow big, second and third generation owners abandon the very strategies that made them successful at the beginning.

When I visit some retail stores especially those that are open late at night, I always think to myself, I wonder if the CEOs of these retail organisations ever shop at their own stores.

I am sure if any of them did, they will be shocked to experience the level of customer service their staff provides their customers.

I will wager the CEO of PC World has never bought computers from his own stores.

He probably just sends his handlers to do his shopping for him, so he never comes face to face with the horrible level of customer service and the almost scandalous incompetence of his store assistants.

If he shops in his store and he allows the status quo to continue, it is not my place to give anyone financial advice, but if I had shares in PC World, I will consider taking it out before it gets too late.

Even NEXT that is winning praises for becoming more profitable than Marks & Spencer can do with better customer service in its stores.

I was at their store in Stratford and Bond Street, trying to find stuff for my son. When I could not find what I was looking for, I looked around for a staff member to seek assistance; not one staff member was around to help me.

I could not find anyone to ask at the Stratford store, neither could I find someone in Bond Street so I walked out and went to GAP where there was someone available to answer my questions.

I bought from there.

This is not an attempt to disparage NEXT; personally, I have nothing against NEXT, PC World or any of the retailers I mentioned.

I am just trying to illustrate a very important point.

In fact, most of NEXT profit did not come from its store sales but from its online and catalogue division that now accounts for over 35 per cent of its business.

What does this mean?

It means NEXT is taking full advantage of the new sales stream brought about by the internet.

Can NEXT current strategy be sustained as a long term retailing strategy and business model?

I doubt that.

Online retailing is picking up.

Many people are indeed taking advantage of the opportunity of doing their shopping from the comfort of their homes. Therefore, any retail organisation making the decision to ramp up its online presence is making the right decision.

However, I see two point for big problems.

The first is the barrier to entry into any online business is very low.

Marks & Spencer or any of NEXT's competitors could hire a smart computer whiz kid who can knock NEXT out of its online dominance in less than 24 hours.

It can be done relatively easily.

The internet is not a business platform; it can only be used as one source of a company's revenue stream.

To depend on it for 35 per cent of your revenue is taunting the gods.

You could wake up one morning, and Google comes up with a new algorithm and your entire business will be gone. It has happened before and it will happen again.

Secondly, the majority of people will still prefer to go to a retail stores to shop.

A lot of people still do not know how to use the internet well.

Many people are still fearful of placing their bank or credit card details online.

The constant report of hacking into the accounts of very big businesses is not helping matters.

Furthermore, shopping is an experience for the majority of people.

Every weekend, the High Streets of big cities are jammed packed with people.

Many of those people do not go to the High Street to shop. They go to experience the atmosphere of being on a High Street or in a shopping mall.

Furthermore, many of the people who go to retail stores go there for a different reason than they did five or ten years ago.

There are two reasons people visit retail outlets these days:

- To buy essentials
- To soak up the experience

Those who go to buy essential can be categorised into:

- Those who lack the ability to use the internet
- Those who prefer to buy directly from shops either because they are afraid to place their card details online or they simply prefer to go directly to the shops
- Those who go to shops even though they could easily buy on the internet but prefer to deal with another human being instead of a computer screen
- Those who go for window shopping; many of these might have seen what they need online but cannot tell the exact size or make, so they go to shops to have the chance to feel the merchandise, and get validation from someone before making their decision to buy online

The second category of shoppers: Those who go to soak up the experience can be broken down in to:

- Those who go simply to window shop with no money or no intention of buying
- Those who just decide to visit a shopping centre as part of their weekend outing
- Those who need to get detailed information before making decision on a purchase
- Those who enjoy the experience of buying in a retail store

What is the common characteristic of people who buy online?

Shoppers who shop online can be categorised as:

- Extremely busy people who almost never get the chance to visit retail outlets
- Shoppers surfing online for the future who then buy impulsively
- Shoppers surfing online for something other than the intension to shop but forced to respond to an ad
- Shoppers who shop online because they have the facilities

Except for those who do not know how to use the internet and who are forced to go to shops, those afraid to place their card details online and those online shoppers who are extremely busy, all other shoppers both online and offline buy for the same two reasons:

For essential use and for the experience

What does this mean for brick and mortar retailers; it means brick and mortar retailers have the ability and opportunity to influence the buying behaviour of shoppers buy tinkering with some little things.

Most surveys have shown that the most commonly bought items online are electronic products.

Richer Sound is aware of this fact, so it has built a business model that appeals to those people in order to lure them from their computers into their stores.

How do they do that?

They do so with knowledgeable staff.

What are the difficult challenges electronic buyers face?

What brand to buy and how to install and use their gadgets.

Richer Sound solves these problems for them by having knowledgeable staff capable of answering customer's queries and helping them make the right decision.

This brings us to a very important point, which is probably the most important point of this entire workbook...*Understanding your target market.*

The Richer Sound Case Study

Richer Sounds sells expensive electronic equipment.

Unfortunately, the more expensive the gadget, the more complicated it is to install and operate.

Why electronic makers make their devices complicated to use and their menus even more complicated to understand is a mystery to me.

But that is for another book.

What is important for you to understand is this…

Richer Sound, understanding the fact that the individual willing to spend thousands for home entertainment does not look forward to spending hours deciding on the best system to buy and the difficulty of setting up the system, *decided to remove this headache and barrier to purchase by providing them knowledgeable staff.*

The Amazon Case Study

One of the main barriers to buying online for most people is fear of receiving the wrong merchandise or not receiving their purchase at all.

Amazon knowing this fully well ensures it provides buyers an ironclad guarantee.

If they do not receive their purchase or if they receive the wrong item and the seller does not make an effort to replace the item, the buyer will receive their money back.

As a seller on Amazon myself, I know Amazon does not take kindly to sellers who do not fulfil their promise to their buyers. They are promptly removed from Amazon sellers list.

Zappos Case Study

Years ago, when someone wanted to buy shoes, they had to go into a shop to try on several pairs before making their choice.

Then online shopping was introduced but the problem with buying shoe online, was even though people knew their size and ordered their size, there was no guarantee that it will fit them.

So when someone ordered a shoe and it did not fit, they had to ship it back at their own expense, costing them time and money.

I know of a situation with a friend of mine who bought shoes online only to discover when she received them that they were not what she wanted.

When she wanted to return it, she discovered it would cost her more to return the shoe than to throw it away.

Needless to say, she will never buy from that company again; neither will any of her friends.

Zappos has a solution to this problem.

When someone buys a shoe from Zappos, if it is not what they like or if it did not fit, they can return the shoes at Zappos expense.

This simple return policy took Zappos from a relatively unknown to one of the biggest online retailer in the world.

Now let us contrast the Richer sound, Amazon or Zappos experience with buying a computer at PC World.

PC World Case Study

Many of us who know how to use computers take for granted the fact that like most electronic devices, it is still not easy to use.

A typical example of this situation is, I was online helping someone to register a company.

While he was online, he kept getting those irritating pop ups that were preventing him from doing the things I was instructing him to do.

The guy had no idea how to get rid of them. He had never in his life heard of popup blockers.

There are many people like him who go into computer stores like PC world to buy computer with no idea the type of computer they need.

In 99.9% of the time, when you enter a PC World store, the store assistant knows **nothing, nada...zip about the devices in the store.**

The best you will get from them is they will read the specs of the products.

When you ask them a question, it is either they do not know or they will mislead you.

The Starting Point Of Store Design and Visual Merchandise Display

Why did I introduce these points?

Certainly not to disparage PC world and praise the other retailers I said good things about. I wanted to make the point about the importance of understanding your target market.

The key to a good store design and an attractive visual merchandising display is first and foremost who you are going to sell to.

Success in designing a beautiful store comes down to three things:

- What you are going to sell
- Who you are going to sell to
- How you are going to sell to them

You might already have a retail store, therefore, already know what you are going to sell.

Even though I will argue you should have gone through this exercise before even stocking and opening your store, I will pretend you know what you are selling.

The question we need to answer here and now is: who you are going to sell to – your target market.

Before going into how to select your target market, I want to firstly to state the reason it is critical that you know who you are going to sell to.

There are several reasons it is essential you have an accurate understanding of who you are going to sell to.

But one of the key reasons is this: the price of a product is determined by who is buying and how it is sold to them.

What this means for you is the price at which you will sell your products, which will ultimately determine your profitability is dependent upon who is buying your products and how you sell it to them.

I told the story of my visit to Harrods for the research of my retail books.

I intimated that instead of Russian oligarch and Saudi Prince, what caught my attention was a bus I had bought for my son in ASDA.

It was the same bus in the same packaging, probably made in the same factory by the same people in China that was sold in Harrods for almost three times the price it was sold for in ASDA.

So why was it that the same bus, in the same factory, made by the same people sold in Harrods almost three times the price it was sold for in ASDA?

The answer is simple: because of who is buying in Harrods and how it is sold to them.

Harrods caters to Royalties, the who-is-who in the world, A-list Hollywood stars and the rich and famous.

While ASDA carters to the person who lives pay check to pay check.

As a result, Harrods store design and visual merchandise display is completely different from that of ASDA's.

This again emphasises the point I keep making about first knowing the who you are going to sell to before deciding on the most appropriate store design that will appeal to those people.

How do you identify who you are going to sell to?

The first step in target market selection is understanding universal human behaviour.

There is the saying that the only constant, is change.

I will argue that the only constant is human behaviour.

Human behaviour has remained the same from the days of Caesar.

Whatever, people do, they do for the same three reasons:

- Sex
- Survival
- Status

As humans, we come hard wired with these tendencies.

When a baby is born, the first things its screams for are air and food… Survival.

Then it seeks affection from its mother…Sex.

Then when it realises that it is not alone vying for his parents love, its start scheming ways of getting one over it semblance and others…Status.

Because of our computers, our smartphones and other gadgets we like to convince ourselves that we have gone past our primitive instincts for:

- Sex
- Survival
- Status

But we have not.

We remain the same creatures we were from birth constantly occupied with the desire for:

- Sex
- Survival
- Status

This workbook is about how to increase retail sales with store design, visual merchandise display and loss prevention.

Therefore, you will be justified to be wondering what this talk is about:

- Sex
- Survival
- Status

Well retail is a business.

Like any other business, the extent to which you are able to sell your products is the extent to which you will succeed.

And the first step in effective marketing is psychographic...*understanding the psychology of the people you want to sell to.*

Therefore understanding the key triggers to why and how people behave is critical for increasing your store sales.

British Tabloid 'The Sun' has the highest circulation of all English Newspapers in the world.

The front page of the sun is constantly covered with naked women displaying their boobs, yet in a conservative country such as The UK, that paper happens to be favourite read in the country.

It's not only men who read 'The Sun'; women also read it in large numbers.

A study about Facebook ads reveal that an image with women's boobs gets equal clicks from both male and female.

Cosmopolitan magazine has the highest circulation of all female magazines in the world.

Here are a few of cosmos headlines:

- His #1 sex wish: 71 guys crave this move…you'll want to drop this magazine and do it on the spot
- 50 Sex Tricks: you will be the first girl naughty enough to try 43 on him
- Best Sex Ever – out gutsy new tips are guaranteed to give him most bad ass orgasm imaginable and you too
- Weird Male behaviour decoded

It is no coincidence that the highest circulated English newspaper and the highest circulated female magazine both constantly have sex and naked women as their cover stories.

It is because sex sells.

Which relates to my accession that the human being came wired from birth to focus on nothing else but:

- Sex
- Survival
- Status

And don't even imagine in your mind that only dumb people read those papers and magazines.

You will be shocked to discover that presidents and wives of presidents top the list of women who read cosmopolitan.

The large majority of guys stumbled upon playboy magazine when they were growing up and had it hidden in a secret location far away from the prying eyes of their parents.

A good understanding of these intricacies of human behaviour provides you an *insight into the thought process of your target market...*

It is the understanding of these intricacies of human behaviour and the superior exploitation of this understanding that helps retailers like Harrods to continue to attract the 'who-is-who' of the world, recession or no recession.

The reason Harrods is able to sell the same crappy made in China bus for three times the price it sells for in ASDA is, Harrods understands that it is not in the bus selling business.

Harrods is in the experience selling business.

Harrods customers do not go to Harrods to buy the crappy made in china bus.

When they pick up the bus and take it to the counter to pay, they are not paying for the bus; they are paying for the *experience* too.

They are paying for the *beautiful store design and attractive visual merchandising display* and they are paying for the *exceptional customer service.*

Remember human behaviour has remained the same since the days of Caesar.

Designing Your Store for Functionality

Functional Store Design Harrods Case Study

Earlier I spoke about leaving NEXT because I could not find a store assistant to assist me.

In Harrods, there are store assistants in every corner of the store, just a finger click away from each and every customer.

They even have play consultants who play with toys with the kids.

Imagine a child walking through the store and a play consultant throws a ball to him.

The child throws it back and he throws it again. Soon they are both bouncing the ball up and down the store.

The child is enjoying it and they are both laughing; do you think that child will want to leave the store without that ball?

Experiences like this are what customers pay for at Harrods.

Functional Store Design Early Learning Centre & Toys R Us Case Study

Early Learning Centre sells children's toys and stuff.

Unlike Harrods where there are play consultants and enough room for the play consultant to play with children, Early Learning Centre stores are like an old soviet dental suit.

Children in the store cannot even turn without bumping into something.

Toys R Us is another toy retailer with stores that are clustered like a soviet dental suit.

At present, they are making profit on the back of the success of products like Lego.

But supermarket and online retailers are beginning to eat into their profitability.

Their profit margin has already declined this year despite the success of the Lego movies and numerous Disney movies.

The reason for this is, Toys R Us, Early Learning Centre and retailers like them do not understand that *they are in the experience business*.

For most retailers, store design is about getting a few builders to knock together shelves and furniture.

However, store design should not start with knocking together shelves and furniture.

The first step needs to be thinking about who we want to attract to the store and design the store to appeal to those types of people.

I have just given you a picture of two extremes, Harrods vs Early Learning Centre & Toys R Us.

While Harrods design its store with its customers in mind, Early Learning Centre and Toys R Us only think about extracting the maximum profitability from every inch of their stores.

But no retailer will be profitable while providing a bad experience to their customers.

You can succeed in making short-term profit but a *bad customer experience* can never be a *profitable long-term strategy*.

Lego do not spend millions to produce Lego movies because they want to get into the movie making business neither do they do it simply to be nice to kids.

Like Harrods, they want to create a positive experience for children and their parents.

When children have a positive affiliation with Lego as a result of watching the movies, it increases their desire for Lego products.

When children go to a toy store that looks and feels like a soviet dental suit, there is no motivation for them to buy other than the fact that they like the characters on sale.

There is a completely different motivation between a child who has spent a few minutes bouncing a ball up and down a store with a play consultant and the child who has to squeeze his way pass the toys on the shelves.

That is the first lesson of designing your retail store: design your store for functionality.

The Benefit of Footfall Counters

Some retail stores are now fitted with footfall counters.

These footfall counters do more than just count the number of customers who enter the store.

They also help with conversion that we will talk about a lot in future sections.

They provide information about the number of shoppers who enter the store… The areas of the stores they visit, the time they spend in each area, time spent queuing at the checkout counter, at customer service counter and the demographic makeup of the shopper.

Importantly, it reveals miss-sales opportunities.

Earlier I mentioned that I was forced to leave NEXT, go out and buy things for my son from GAP because I could not find a sales assistant to help me, in two NEXT stores.

That was missed sales opportunity for NEXT.

If they had installed the technology, or if they have it, if someone is actually monitoring it and using the data, they will notice the number of sales opportunities they miss from the likes of people like me.

The same goes for PC world.

I have written about my experience in PC World on many occasions.

I have said the only reason I went to PC World, it was the only store in my area that had the HP ink for my printer.

When you enter a PC World and ask the store assistants for information, they will either have no idea of what you are talking about or they will mislead you.

And when you go to the checkout, you will stand in the queue waiting to be served while a few meters from you, staff member chats away about the Manchester derby.

Now that I no longer have that printer, you will need a tow truck to tow me to into a PC world store.

With fierce competition on the internet, imagine the amount of profit PC World and retailers like it are leaving on the table because they do not design their stores with us the customers in mind.

Imagine if they had a footfall technology and someone was actually watching it and making management decisions based on the data…imagine the difference it will make to their profitability.

The Magic Mirror

There is also a really cool piece of technology called the *Magic Mirror*.

This is an essential bit of software mostly for clothing retailers. However, the Germans have now designed one that is suitable for any type of retailer.

It allows you to try virtual designs of clothes without actually trying them on.

Someone could go into a retail store, choose a trouser, and the mirror will show them various options of shirts, t-shirts, shoes, trainers, jacket, coat glasses socks and every other accessory that matches that trouser.

They can immediately send images to families and friends to gauge their opinion.

A man no longer has to endure the torture of waiting outside the fitting room while their spouse tries on millions of dresses.

She can simply choose it and send it to him on his phone, for confirmation.

This magic mirror does not only make the shopping experience pleasant and stress free for the customer, it also leads to upsell and impulse buying.

When customers try different types of accessories, there is a high chance of them buying a few of them.

That individual might come into your store with the intention of buying a pair of jeans and he might walk out with shirt, t-shirt, trainers etc.

However, the above is only possible if you design functionality into your retail store design. That is if you deliberately purchase those technologies to enhance your customer experience.

Yes, at the planning stage of the design, a conscious decision must be made as to who you want to sell to and how you want to sell to them.

Workshop

1. Why do you think shoppers come to your store?

___

___

___

2. Do shoppers have reason to remain for long in your store?

___

___

___

3. What experience do shoppers have when they visit your store?

___

___

___

4. What exactly is it are you selling to your customer?

___

___

___

5. What do you think your customers are buying from you?

_____

_____

_____

6. Are they persuaded to buy from you because of your store design and visual merchandise display?

_____

_____

_____

7. As the owner or senior management of the store, do you know with certainty the experience shoppers have in your store or were you told by a research firms?

_____

_____

_____

8. What percentage of your customers return to your store?

_____

_____

_____

9. Do you strategically choreograph your sales process?

_____

_____

_____

10. Do you use technology to monitor the activities of customers in your store?

_____

_____

_____

How Do You Select Your Target Audience: Who Are You Going To Sell To?

When lingerie retailer La Senza went into administration, I thought, and still believe they went into administration because they changed the design of their lingerie.

I shopped at La Senza for my other half.

At one point, I even worked for La Senza in loss prevention capacity.

When I shopped or worked at La Senza, it sold really beautiful stuff.

Then its designers decided to change to Bridget Jones design.

This I believe was the cause of La Senza troubles…the fact that it strayed away from its target market.

The same thing keeps happening over and over with retailers that go bust or into administration. They have no demographic appeal.

It's amazing to see the concept of good demographic identification at work in the supermarkets.

You visit ASDA and you see a completely different demographic makeup of customers than you will find in Tesco, Morrisons or Sainsbury.

Few of the ways supermarkets do their target market selection is the location of their store, their product range and their marketing communications.

We will address communication later in the workbook, but I want to stick to criterion for effective target market selection, at this point.

I will go a bit into universal marketing and target market selection instead of just focusing on selecting retail customers.

I will later explain the concept as it applies to the retail industry.

Let us say you agree with me about the importance of good target market segmentation, what are the best ways of slicing and dicing the population of your city or country, to choose the right segment to serve?

There are lots of ways of breaking down or segmenting your target market.

Here are just two of the most common target market segments:
- By Demographics
- By Preference or Interest

Segment Category One: Demographics

There are six demographic categories:
- Income Level
- Age
- Gender
- Education/Technical Level
- Ethnic/Culture
- Location

Segment Category 2: Preferences or Interests

You could segment by various interests and hobbies in which people engage.

These include:

- Hobbies – art, trains, computer games, gardening or crafts
- Sports – fishing, golf or football
- Health – conventional medicine, alternative medicine, diet, exercise or chemicals
- Education – training programs, books, computers or videos
- Leisure Activities – hiking, theatre, reading, games or vacations
- Causes – environmental, social or political

The Best Target Market Categories

The best target market categories are your past and present customers.

Your past and present customers, who are the most neglected, are usually the most productive of any target market.

Your past and present customers have already bought from you. They already trust you. Therefore, they are the easiest group to sell to.

The thing about your past and present customers you know who they are.

You know a lot of things about them that you can use as a basis for choosing your target market.

However, ask yourself this question as you read this workbook: Do you know anything about your past and present customers?

Do you even capture details of shoppers who buy from you?

This is where the process of target market segmentation starts.

You cannot make accurate decisions without accurate information.

An accurate decision in this instant means having comprehensive data of your current customers. It will provide you with information of the types of people to pursue.

These days the mechanism for capturing that type of information can range from something as simple as having a loyalty program to using sophisticated technology to slice and dice your customers.

Capturing Details of:

- What someone bought at your store
- The frequency with which they buy
- The monetary value of their purchase
- The pattern of purchase

Such data will give you a good indication of the types of people who shop at your store and provide clues of the types of prospects to seek.

When you identify your target, how do you communicate with them in order for them to know that they are the ones you are trying to attract to your store?

This is the subject of the next section.

Workshop

1. Do you know your target market?

_____

_____

_____

2. Have you segmented your target market to enable you communicate with them effectively?

_____

_____

_____

3. What experience do shoppers have when they visit your store?

_____

_____

_____

4. Do you have an accurate database of your current customers?

_____

_____

_____

5. What incentive do you give your customers to persuade them to give you their personal details?

_____

_____

_____

Crafting Your Marketing Message: What Are You Going to Sell to Them

After you have identified your target market, how do you get them into your store?

The process for getting them into your store is called 'crafting' your marketing message.

What is your marketing message?

Your marketing message is your point of differentiation and your offer.

The first important point about a marketing message is, it can never be effective if it is not done from your prospect or customer perspective.

You constantly need to ask the question: what's in it for my prospect or customer…not what's in it for me.

The starting point for crafting a compelling marketing message is asking the question; why do people buy or do not buy your product or service.

According to the legendary marketer Jay Conrad Levinson, people buy for 50 different reasons.

Understanding some of those reasons will enable you create a marketing message that resonates with your target market.

People buy:

1. To make more money – even though it can't buy happiness
2. To become more comfortable, even a bit more
3. To attract praise – because almost everybody loves it
4. To increase enjoyment – of life, of business, of virtually anything
5. To possess things of beauty – because they nourish the soul
6. To avoid criticism – which nobody wants
7. To make their work easier – a constant need for too many people
8. To speed up their work – because people know that time is precious
9. To keep up with the Joneses – there are Joneses in everybody's life
10. To feel opulent – a rare, but valid reason to make a purchase
11. To look younger – due to the reverence placed upon youthfulness
12. To become more efficient – because efficiency saves time
13. To buy friendship – I didn't know it's for sale, but it often is
14. To avoid effort – because nobody loves to work too hard
15. To escape or avoid pain – which is an easy path to making a sale
16. To protect their possessions – because they worked hard to get them
17. To be in style – because few people enjoy being out of style
18. To avoid trouble – because trouble is never a joy

19. To access opportunities – because they open the doors to good things
20. To express love – one of the noblest reasons to make any purchase
21. To be entertained – because entertainment is usually fun
22. To be organized – because order makes life simpler
23. To feel safe – because security is a basic human need
24. To conserve energy – their own or their planet's sources of energy
25. To be accepted – because that means security as well as love
26. To save time — because they know time is more valuable than money
27. To become more fit and healthy — seems to me that's an easy sale
28. To attract the opposite sex – never undermine the power of love
29. To protect their family – tapping into another basic human need
30. To emulate others – because the world is teeming with role models
31. To protect their reputation – because they worked hard to build it
32. To feel superior – this is why status symbols are sought after
33. To be trendy – because they know their friends will notice
34. To be excited – because people need excitement in a humdrum life

35. To communicate better—because they want to be understood
36. To preserve the environment – giving rise to cause-related marketing
37. To satisfy an impulse – a basic reason behind a multitude of purchases
38. To save money – the most important reason for 14% of the population
39. To be cleaner – because unclean often goes with unhealthy and unloved
40. To be popular – because inclusion beats exclusion every time
41. To satisfy curiosity – it killed the cat but motivates the sale
42. To satisfy their appetite – because hunger is not a good thing
43. To be individual – because all of us are, and some of us need assurance
44. To escape stress – need I explain?
45. To gain convenience – because simplicity makes life easier
46. To be informed – because it's no joy to be perceived as ignorant
47. To give to others – another way you can nourish your soul
48. To feel younger – because that equates to vitality and energy
49. To pursue a hobby – because all work and no play etc. etc. etc.
50. To leave a legacy – because that's a way to live forever

As you noticed from the above list, many of the reasons for which people buy are emotional.

It goes back to the point about:

- Sex
- Survival
- Status

We are all emotional beings.

Therefore, your marketing message needs to appeal more to the emotion than logic.

What are the reasons people don't buy?

Why do shoppers enter your store and leave without buying?

Or they visit your website, get all the way to the shopping cart and abandon the shopping?

According to legendary copywriter Gary Bencivenca, there are five reasons people don't buy or what he called universal objections:

- No time
- No interest
- No perceived difference
- No belief
- No decision

When you send out your marketing leaflet, your social media post or create your website, these are the five reasons people will not respond to them.

Now instead of thinking of clever ways of tricking them into buying from you, you need be thinking of ways of addressing all five of those objections.

So how do you address these objections?

You do that by using the Bencivenga Persuasion Equation.

The Bencivenga Persuasion Equation was developed by Gary Bencivenga to counter buying objections.

It (The Bencivenga persuasion equation) goes like this:

> **Problem + Promise + Proof + Preposition = Persuasion**

The problem

The fact that you are in the retail business does not make your business different from any other business.

As a business, you are solving problems.

When someone comes into your retail store to buy a suit, they are buying it because they need the suit to solve a problem.

> They might need the suit:
> - To go for a dinner
> - To go on a date
> - To go for a job interview
> - To attend a business meeting

All of these are problems the suit is solving.

And problem is market.

As long as there is a desire, want or need for your product, there is a problem that needs a solution.

So what you need to ask yourself is: what problem is my product solving.

This question is especially important for new or existing retailers.

I always have this discussion with business owners when they ask me to help them market their products.

Case Study

The most interesting conversations I have are with professionals.

A lawyer calls me and say he wants to open a law firm and need help with attracting clients.

When I ask what problems is he going to be solving in the legal marketplace, nine out of ten of the times he cannot give me a concrete answer.

My conversation with him usually go like this:

Dude, I can see there are already fifty lawyers in your town, twenty immigration lawyers and you are an immigration lawyer, why should someone come to your firm instead of one of the other existing firms?

The answer is almost always: I am going to provide personal service bla bla bla… do you think the existing immigration lawyers do not provide personal service?

Or do you think when someone goes to their firm they will say something like: we provide crappy service but you see there is a new firm across the road that provides personal service.

We need something other than personal service to sell them.

In most instances, they have nothing else to sell.

As you read this, you want to ask yourself, what problem does your product solve?

A lady going into a lingerie store might need the lingerie to go on a date.

By asking a few questions, a store assistant will know the reason she needs the lingerie therefore, will know the type to sell to her.

Firstly, going through the process will make the difference between window-shopping and purchase and it could lead to upsell.

The Promise

The next step in the persuasion equation is your promise.

What promise can you make to your target market and customers to solve their problems?

Taking into account the reasons people buy – fast, convenient, exclusive etc.

Earlier we spoke about Tesco adding extra checkout counters to speed up the checkout process.

This is Tesco promising the customer that you can come into our store, get want you want and leave within minutes.

Pret a Manger is a food retailer who promised to get customer out of the store under five minutes.

What is your equivalent of "fresh hot pizza delivered in 30 minutes"?

The Proof

People are used to be given promises that are not kept.

So what proof can you provide to back up your claims?

Let's take the Tesco scenario as an example again.

Placing additional checkout counters in Tesco stores is a proof to Tesco's customers that the retailer is serious about increasing speed at the checkout.

The Offer

The forth element of the equation is your offer.

You have made a promise and provided proof to back up your offer, what type of offer can you provide them to entice them to enter your store?

Your offer could be your price, guarantee or your payment terms.

One of the strategies Next used to entice its customers was to provide them store card…literally giving them money with which to buy their products.

When you have these four elements in your marketing message or campaign, you increase the likelihood of persuading your customers and target market to visit your store regularly.

> *Remember its all about compassion for the customer, listening to the voice of the customer and give them what they want.*

So what is your marketing message and why is it important for attracting customers to your store?

Your marketing message is basically your competitive advantage.

What is your competitive advantage?

Your competitive advantage is a benefit you have that your competitors don't.

The source of the advantage is something your business does that is distinctive and difficult to replicate.

Walmart (ASDA) is considered the cheapest supermarket. The reason Walmart is able to maintain its position as the cheapest supermarket is, it has the most efficient supply chain system in the retail industry.

Walmart supply chain moves like a clockwork. No other retailer have been able to match their efficiency and no other retailer might ever be able to.

That is their competitive advantage.

Competitive advantage comes from providing unique value, by drawing on special areas of talent and strengths.

Your competitive advantage is core competencies you develop that enable you to serve your customers better than your competitors.

Your core competencies are a unique set of capabilities, skills and expertise you develop in key areas such as:

- Superior quality
- Innovation
- Customer service
- Team building
- Responsiveness
- Flexibility

They can also be the leveraging of proprietary technologies, information, relationships, and unique operating methods that provide the product that customers value and want to buy.

Creating an effective competitive advantage is very critical for your business because there is no greater way to grow your business quickly than to occupy a strategic position in the marketplace.

Competition between businesses is as much a race for competent mastery as it is for market position, market power and profits.

Developing a competitive advantage is like competing in a miss world beauty competition.

The audience watching have in their heads who they think is going to win, the media have their own favourite yet some girl from some obscure country stuns everyone by winning the crown.

How did it happen?

She had a uniqueness about her that went unnoticed by all, except the judges.

Richer Sound has uniqueness about it that is only visible to its customers.

Harrods remains the favourite shopping place for the rich and famous because it has a uniqueness about it that is only visible to its high flying customers.

Your store needs to have a uniqueness about it that is only visible to your target market.

You need to be able to speak to them with your message in a way that only they can understand.

When I spoke about the Gary Bencivenga equation, I revealed the fact that problem is market.

As a business, you need to have a reason for your existence.

Your existence has to have something to do with filling a gap in your marketplace or solving a pressing problem.

Domino pizza solves the problem of getting food to hungry college students who wanted food fast.

Fedx solved the problem of getting mail to customers overnight and now the same day.

Google helps us to find almost any information instantly. We no longer need to go to the library to search.

Facebook solve the problem of connecting people.

GAP was established to fill a gap in the clothing market.

TK Maxx allows customers the chance to buy branded clothes at reasonable price.

- Why does your store exist?
- What problem is your store solving?
- What gap is your store filling in the retail market?

Creating an effective USP: Words That Sell

Many retailers avoid or struggle to create a USP because they find it difficult to differentiate themselves from their competitors.

The majority of retailers are incapable of clearly articulating what makes them different from their competitor.

Let me say this from the word go; *USP is something you position in the minds of your customers or prospects.*

It does not necessarily have to be something tangible, it just has to be something they believe about your business.

In order to be able to create a good USP, you need to be able to answer two questions:

- Question number one: why do you exist in your marketplace?
- Question number two: What problem are you solving in your marketplace?

Remember what I said previously, problem is market. When there is no problem, there is no market.

In order to be able to answer the questions: why do you exist and what problem are you solving in your marketing place, you need to be able to answer the question:

What does my customer want?

This is how to go about the process:

Imagine your store is a theatre stage and you can shine the spotlight on a single person or object, what will you shine it on?

There are four possible things you could shine the spotlight on:

- You
- Your business
- Your product
- Your customer

What do the majority of retailers do? They shine the spotlight on themselves or their products.

However, in order to create an effective marketing message, the spotlight has to be shone on your customers.

Your entire focus has to be what do your customers want?

There needs to be a straight line between the customer's wants and your offer.

How do you do that?

Offer creation Process: Step One

You do that by finding out what your customer wants, needs and desires are.

You can do that by researching your market.

It's amazing how many retailers know nothing about their customers.

Let me give you a secret, if you want to know what your customer, thinks, feels, wants, needs and desires, check out your most successful competitors.

But here is a word of caution, don't check out what they are doing now, check out what they did from the start.

When many retailers become successful, they drop the ball and stop doing the things that made them successful.

At the start of many retail businesses, the founders did the right things to grow the business.

However, as they grow bigger, they bring in professional Harvey business graduates who stray 360 degrees from the things that made them successful.

Offer Creation Process: Step Two

The next step in your offer creation is to check out trade magazines.

Offer Creation Process: Step Three

Check out social media and online forums to see what your customers are posting.

Offer Creation Process: Step Four

Check out other purchases your customers made. What they bought previously says a lot about them.

After you gather this intelligence, the next step in the process is to craft your marketing message.

This is the offer creation equation:

> The product + the time and effort they're going to put in + the three big benefit-oriented results that they're going to get.

This is an explanation of the formula:

The information in this book is a transcript of a workshop.

At the end of the workshop, the primary benefit for attendees is they will be able to increase their store sales.

The secondary benefit is:

- They will learn how to attract customers to their store
- They will learn how to design their store well
- They will learn how to create an attractive visual merchandise display
- They will learn how to reduce their shrinkage and increase their profit margin

However, the title of the program is 'how to increase retail sales' because I know in the final analysis, the desire of the attendees is not to learn how to do all of the secondary things but to increase their sales.

Hence I named the workshop, How to Increase Retail Sales to appeal to their primary objective.

Your message needs to be direct, clear, emotional, compelling and so benefit and result-oriented that it literally stops your customers, in their tracks, and gets them to take action.

There needs to be a direct connection between the desire of your prospect, their emotional desire and the result or the outcome and the benefit that your product offers.

That connection has to be perfect and the closer it is the better.

The more of a connection you hit, the more you draw your prospects in and the more you drive them to take action.

Furthermore, you need to ensure that your message appeals to the three brains:

- The logical brain
- The physical brain
- The emotional brain

But the emotional part of your message has to be the most dominant because our emotional brain is the most dominant of the three.

What you are looking for in your marketing message is emotional impact not so much intellectual impact.

What you are looking for is *gut-level emotion that is specific, instant, new, different, better, unusual or dramatic.*

According to Conrad Levin people do not buy the products in your store; they buy the following:

1. Solutions to their problems
2. Freedom from pain
3. Promises you make
4. Wealth, safety, success, security, love and acceptance
5. Your guarantee, reputation and good name
6. Other people's opinions of your business
7. Believable claims, not simply honest claims.
8. Brand names over strange names
9. Easy access to information offered by your web site
10. The consistency they've seen you exhibit.
11. The stature of the media in which you market
12. The professionalism of your marketing materials
13. Value, which is not the same as price
14. Freedom from risk, granted by your warranty
15. Convenience in purchasing
16. Neatness and assume that's how you do business
17. Honesty for one dishonest word means no sale
18. Speedy delivery

What people don't buy are the following:

1. Fancy adjectives
2. Exaggerated claims.
3. Clever headlines
4. Special effects
5. Marketing that screams
6. Marketing that even hints at amateurishness

The following are the things people want. They want to be:

- Happy
- Safe
- Successful
- Wealthy
- Liked
- Loved
- Be pain free
- Eat tasty foods, and
- Have fun
- Have a sense of purpose

Most businesses often confuse features with benefits. It's important to differentiate between them:

- Features are the things inherent in your product
- Benefits are what the buyer gets from your product

Another angle to USP creation is the use of your personal story.

There is the saying in marketing that fact tells but story sells.

As kids we were conditioned to love stories.

Our parents read bed side stories to us.

At school, our very first lessons were all stories.

That early conditioning have stuck with us even in adulthood.

All religious books are written in the form of stories – think about the amount of people who have some type of faith, that's the power of good story telling.

So you can use your personal story as an effective USP.

We have learnt in previous sections that people buy emotionally but justify their decisions logically.

A well-crafted story can create affinity and bonding with your market faster than any other marketing tool you might want to deploy.

The first time president Barack Obama, spoke at the Democratic National Convention, he told the story of how his father left from Africa to US, how he met his mother and how he witnessed his mother die while she argue with insurance companies over treatments and entitlement.

His story is not only his story, it is the story of many African-Americans, Latinos and foreign born white Americans who form the core of his constituent.

When you effectively tell stories that touch people's hearts, it is very easy to touch their wallets.

In Dr. Robert Chadini's book influence, he outlined 'like' as a key factor of influence.

People buy from people they like and trust.

When you get people to believe you are like them, there is a high possibility they will want to do business with you.

How to Use Your Story As a USP

In order to use your story as your USP, it has to follow a specific structure.

The great mythologist Joseph Campbell studied mythologies in different parts of the world. In his years of study, he discovered that there were common structures that all mythologies followed no matter the place and culture.

That structure formed the core of his book The Hero's Journey.

This is the structure of a typical USP story structure:

- Your story has to start from your struggle…
- Then your revelation or realisation…
- Then your struggle to get the epiphany…
- Then the breakthrough…
- Then how you taught others who worked for you and, they tried it and it worked for them.

So its like:

- Here is where I was…
- Then I received the calling…
- I took action but it was difficult…
- Then I finally made a breakthrough…
- When it worked for me, I showed it to others, it worked for them too…
- Then I systematised the process, now I want to show you how to use the system to realise your own dream.

When you create a conversion story using the above formula, you are likely to resonate with your market.

As a retailer, you might think to yourself, this type of stuff does not apply to me.

But before you dismiss it, walk around the shopping centre in your town, or go to different supermarkets and see if it is the same types of people entering every store.

The most successful retailers understand this formula because it is what they use to appeal to different segments of the market.

The Body Shop is the best example of someone using their personal story to develop their brand.

Dame Anita Roddick branded the Body Shop in her image.

While I was conducting the research for this workbook, I took a break to eat and check my email. I saw this email from Seth Godin the bestselling author of multiple marketing books including Purple Cow.

This is what the email said:

"Its a story. About money.

Money isn't real. It's a method of exchange, a unit we exchange for something we actually need or value. It has worth because we agree what it can be exchanged for.

But there's something far more powerful going on here.

We don't actually agree, because each person's evaluation of money is based on the stories we tell ourselves about it.

Our bank balance is merely a number, bits represented on a screen, but it's also a signal and symptom. We tell ourselves a story about how we got that money, what it says about us, what we're going to do with it and how other people judge us. We tell ourselves a story about how it might grow, and more vividly, how that money might disappear or shrink or be taken away.

And those stories, those very powerful unstated stories, impact the narrative of just about everything else we do.

So yes, there's money. But before there's money, there's a story. It turns out that once you change the story, the money changes too".

I could not have made a better case for using your story as a USP.

What is an offer?

Your offer is what you use to entice your customer to buy your product.

It is basically how you communicate your unique selling preposition to your prospects to entice them to buy from you as opposed to your competitor.

One of the difficulties of selling is making your prospect understand the value of your product to them.

Sometimes you might have a unique product that you might think to yourself, this is slam dunk, anyone who sees or hears about my product will want it.

However, when the product is brought to the market, you struggle to sell it because people do not see the value that you see in it.

I used the words need and want interchangeably and deliberately because as entrepreneurs, many of us get into the habit of selling people things because we think they need it.

Unless you have a grocery store in the middle of Sahara Desert, everything you are selling is a want not a need.

And most of the times, people don't buy what they need, they what they want.

When I consult professionals and point this fact out to them, they are always surprise at that fact that people do not want to use their services even though they need it.

If everyone was buying what they really needed, no one will splash out one million pounds to buy a Bugatti or Ferrari.

Does someone really need a Bugatti?

No they want it.

So why do they buy it?

People buy what they want not what they need.

It all comes down to understanding human psychology when constructing your offer.

What are the Elements of a Good Offer?

According to Mary Ellen Tribby founder and CEO of Working Moms Only.com, a good offer must pass the following litmus test:

1. It has to be specific – with your prospect understanding exactly what they get and how to get it
2. It has to be exclusive – it has to be made for a select few not to everyone
3. It has to be valuable – your prospects need to perceive your offer as valuable to them
4. It has to be unique – your offer needs to be available only through your business
5. It has to be useful – your offer can be exclusive, but unless it's unique, it's not useful.
6. It has to be relevant-your prospects need to actually want what you are offering them
7. It has to be plausible – some offers sound too good to be true; that sometimes will make you look a little silly.
8. It has to be easy to acquire – make sure you are offering to let them buy throughout the copy. Make sure your 800 numbers are clear. Make sure your links are working, all those kinds of things.
9. It has to be urgent – you need to have a deadline or early bird special
10. It must have a guarantee – this, without a doubt, strengthens your offer.

Why You Need To Conduct a Competitive Analysis

In the words of Benjamin Gilad "Behind every successful strategy, there has been a tireless effort to collect intelligence".

Strategy is concerned with what your business wants to do in the world.

Competitive intelligence focuses on what the world wants to do to your business.

As a business consultant, I constantly, speak to new entrepreneurs who will swear that they have no competition.

If your retail store has no competitor, it either means it is not a viable business or you have not conducted a competitive analysis. Every business has a competitor either directly or indirectly.

Your competitor might be other retailers who are trying to eat your lunch or other products and services competing for your prospect's money.

Therefore, it is essential that you understand who and what you are up against in order to be able to craft an effective offer.

Sun Tzu the great Chinese military strategist wrote Art of War:

> *"—If you are ignorant of both your enemy and yourself, then you are a fool and certain to be defeated in every battle.*
>
> *—If you know yourself, but not your enemy, for every battle won, you will suffer a loss.*
>
> *—If you know your enemy and yourself, you will win every battle".*

At the least, you should know your competitors offer because that will enable you craft an effective counter offer.

Conducting Competitive Analyses

You could purchase your competitors products to familiarise yourself with their sales process and offer.

Get in their mailing list to study their communication strategies, their promotions and announcements.

Go into their stores to buy and gauge the level of customer service you receive.

Then return the products at different intervals to gauge the level of service you receive when you make returns.

These are suggestions that might affront you.

You might think to yourself; how can I buy my competitor's products?

If your competitors get their hands on this training, they may be the ones buying your product to spy on you and reverse engineer your offer.

You should check the online collateral of your top ten competitors.

Check their websites, their website copies, their links on every page and their different websites.

Conduct keyword searches on the major search engines and click on the first ten organic results and the first ten paid results.

Go to each of those websites landing pages, spy on their keywords, sales funnel and offers.

Competitive analysis is a tedious process. It requires a lot of work.

I am not suggesting as the owner of the business you conduct it yourself, ideally, you might want to partake in many of these processes yourself.

What is important for you is to understand the process. Ensure someone in your organisation is doing it and check to ensure it is completed.

After you have determined your competitors offer, you now assess your own logistic and delivery strength to ascertain if you have the resources to match or exceed their offer.

I must repeat this point; problem is market.

Your offer has to be about the market not about you or your competitors.

Your competitors offers might not take into account the wants and desires of the market.

So if you blindly follow them, you will end up in the same dish as them.

Many large retailers are guilty of this…They are completely out of touch with their customers.

Your process should be to understand the problems i.e. wants and desires of your customers.

Spy on your competitors to see how they are satisfying the wants of the market.

Assess your own resources to see if you could either match or exceed their offers.

Armed with this information you can now craft an offer that directly speaks to your prospects.

Remove Obstacles to Purchase

The one thing that people lack the most in the current marketplace is trust.

The barrier to entry into the retail marketplace has been lowered.

At present anyone with an internet connection can run a multimillion pound retail operation.

However, because of the ease of entry into the retail market, the quality of both product and service has fallen and people know this.

I told the story of a friend of mine who bought a shoe online when the shoe arrived it was not what she ordered. When she checked out the return policy, she quickly came to the conclusion it was cheaper to bin the shoe than to return it.

Consequently, you need to understand that people are naturally sceptical these days, which is why when you are constructing your offer, you need to anticipate their objections and address them in your offer.

The following are the fears people have that prevent them from purchasing any product:

- Fear of financial loss
- Fear of loss of "face"
- Fear of loss of time
- Fear of inconvenience
- Fear of hassle or intimidation
- Fear of unsatisfactory results
- Fear of disappointment and frustration

To reduce these fears, you need to use the strongest and boldest guarantee possible. Demonstrate to them that you are taking all of the risk.

The following are few of the more effective risk reversal strategies:

- Conditional money back guarantee
- Unconditional money back guarantee
- Money-back plus (something in addition)
- Double-your-money-back
- Performance-based guarantee
- Time-based guarantee
- Lifetime guarantee
- Competitor challenge

The following are the most effective terminologies to use:

- 100% Money-Back Guarantee
- 100% Satisfaction
- No Questions Asked
- No Hassles
- Better Than Risk-Free
- "We'll Buy It Back!"
- "Try It Before You Decide"

Delay is the death of any sales, therefore, in your offer, you need to motivate your prospects into immediate action.

The following are the best words and phrases to use to induce quick action:

- Urgent or scarce
- Limited Discount
- Limited Supply
- Limited Spots
- Pending Price Increase
- Market Test
- Fast-Action Bonuses
- Deadline
- Act now or lose…

In your offer, you need to tell them exactly what you want them to do.

People usually say they don't like being patronised. However, there is lots of evidence to the contrary.

The majority of people like to be led, so forget the stuff of people don't like being patronised.

If you want them to take a certain action, patronise them.

Tell them exactly what action you like them to take in your offer.

Say they came to your online store; ensure in your sales process, you tell them exactly what to do and what to expect.

For example, tell them something like, grab your copy now.

Click on the 'Add To Cart Button Below'. You will be taken immediately to our secure payment form.

Immediately after you enter your information and press the 'Submit Button', you will be given access to…

So, go ahead, click the 'Add –to-Cart Button below'… and gain immediate access to your stuff.

You can apply similar strategy to customers entering your store.

As we have already pointed out, you can use your store design and visual display to get your customers to take the action you like them to take when they are in your store.

However, without sounding like a used car salesman, you can also talk them into taking the action you like them to take when they are in your store.

It is about you understanding that you can get people to do the things you like them to do if you ask them in a certain way.

Once you have identified your USP and crafted your offer, you are ready go ahead and create your marketing message.

Remember that your marketing message is the combination of your USP and your offer.

Workshop

1. Why do you exist as a business, what gap are you trying to fill in the retail marketplace with your store?

_____

_____

_____

2. What is your marketing message: cheap, exclusive or expensive? What is your irresistible offer?

_____

_____

_____

3. What is your equivalent of "fresh hot pizza delivered in 30 minutes"?

_____

_____

_____

4. What promise can you make to your target market and customers to solve their problems?

_____

_____

_____

5. So what proof can you provide to back up your claim?

_____

_____

_____

6. What problem does my product solve?

_____

_____

_____

7. What is your equivalent of "fresh hot pizza delivered in 30 minutes"?

_____

_____

_____

8. Do you conduct competitive analysis to understand your customers?

_____

_____

_____

9. What is your personal story, can you use it as your USP?

_____

_____

_____

10. Do you make strong offers to entice customers into your store?

_____

_____

_____

Your Marketing Media: How Are You Going to Sell to Them?

Over the last few months, I have attended several business shows and exhibitions around London.

As a marketing consultant, when I walked around the stands, I could not stop myself from scanning for good headlines and taglines that I could whip-up for my own promotion.

I entered different stands and spoke to exhibitors, hoping they would try selling me their products or services so I could learn their sales pitch.

However, almost without fail, I noticed many of the exhibitors just showed up as a tick box exercise in order to convince themselves that they have done some form of marketing for the year.

Exhibition stands are not particularly cheap; the least one can get them for is £3000. But as I walked around, I kept thinking to myself, some entrepreneur has wasted £3000 of his hard earn money in order to make himself feel good that he had done some type of marketing.

For many of the staff members, it's an opportunity to get out of the office and from the prying eyes of their bosses.

Or at the very least, a chance to be seen doing something.

Moreover, when it's time for that long awaited promotion, they could claim that they had made a presentation at the exhibition never mind the fact that they did not make a single sale.

Probably in nine out of 10 of the stands, I had to enter the stand to ask what they did exactly, because it was not evident from just looking at the stands.

Some of them had the names of their company written in large lettering as if their companies were Coca Cola or Nike.

I also observed many companies that took presentation and workshop spots hired presenters who could be bothered to practice the scripts to do the presentations on their behalf.

However, the biggest of all problems I noticed was, not a single person tried to close me.

They were all concerned with collecting my details and promising to contact after the show instead of trying to close me right there and then.

So why did many of those companies including some big players make such colossal errors?

There are two answers to this question.

The first is this, for many businesses, marketing means placing an ad in the newspapers, radio, yellow pages or in this case an exhibition.

Secondly, not a lot of businesses follow the steps we have outlined so far to, first craft their marketing message; identify their target market before considering the media through which to channel their marketing message.

Marketing media: newspapers, magazines, TV, radio or social media are just conduits through which you can channel your marketing message.

Placing the wrong marketing massage in front of the wrong audience is a waste of resources. Equally so, placing a great marketing message in the wrong media is a waste of resources.

What do I mean by this?

At present, many retail organisations are jumping on to the social media bandwagon and the social media platform of choice is, Facebook.

The assumption is that everyone has a Facebook account.

Firstly, that assumption is false; not everyone has a Facebook account.

Secondly, not everyone with a Facebook account is actually active on Facebook.

What this means, is that as a retailer, if you simply place your promotional campaign on Facebook with the assumption that it will be seen by your target market, you could be wasting your resources.

This is the reason why the first two steps were very critical.

By first knowing who you want to sell to and what you are going to sell to them, you will be able to choose accurately, the right media through which to channel your marketing message.

If in the process of identifying your target market, you realise that the majority of them hangout on Twitter or LinkedIn rather than Facebook, you could broadcast your marketing message on Twitter or LinkedIn instead of Facebook.

This goes for any other marketing channel you may choose to use.

The goal needs to be to hit your target market.

This is a very critical point because this is where the rubber meets the road when it comes to attracting customers to your store.

> ***The key phrase here is, know thy customer***

You need to know where your customers hangout if you are to reach them quickly and cheaply. This is why the three-step process is very important.

If you want to run a successful marketing campaign, you will need to follow the steps exactly as I have outlined them in this workbook.

- Identify your target market
- Create an effective marketing message

And then

- Select the right media through which to channel the marketing message

In some instances, you could change the order of steps one and two.

You could spot a market or opportunity and determine you are in the position to fill that gap so you can now design an effective marketing message to appeal to that market.

However, for retailers who are already in existence and are seeking to attract more customers, since you already know what you are selling, all you need to do is plan an effective marketing message; select a segment of your market and select the right media through which to channel that marketing message.

The Various Types of Marketing Media

What are the various types of marketing channels?

They are:

Offline media:
- Newspapers & Magazines
- TV & Radio
- Billboard
- Events
- Product giveaways
- Discount coupons
- Postal and leaflets
- Direct mail

Online media:
- Social media
- Your website
- Blog
- Pop Ups
- Banner ad
- Video sites
- Article directories

By today's standard, many of the offline media have become expensive.

Customers are becoming accustomed to freebies.

Social media one of the most powerful marketing tools of our generation is somewhat free and these days anyone could build a website for free.

This is a good and a bad news.

The good news is the barrier to entry into any business has lowered considerably.

Anyone can wake up in the middle of the night, think of a business and start the business right on the spot.

Well sort of.

I said sort of, because anyone who puts up a website can now claim to be in business.

Never mind that he could not have a single customer or any valuable product or service to sell.

Never the less it's good news for anyone with the ability to take advantage of the ease with which things can be done now.

The bad news is competition is becoming steeper, again sort off.

Almost every industry is getting overcrowded.

Even professional services once owned by a handful of professionals with the resources to establish their own business are slowly becoming overcrowded.

That, as lots of professionals flock to establish their own businesses because they feel all they need to market their businesses is a website or social media.

These days, anyone with an internet connection can run a multi-billion pound retail operation. They do not even need an inventory.

All they need is an internet connection and a laptop once they can get a fulfilment company to fulfil their orders.

As a retailer, I need you to get this.

This is another very important fact I need you to take from this workbook.

> Your competitors have changed.

You are no longer competing with retailers you once considered your competitors.

Aside from other retailers, you are now competing with *a guy, in fact, many guys sat in their rooms with their laptops selling exactly what you are selling and on many occasions, at one tenth of your price.*

You are competing against a bloke in India or China whose name you do not even know.

When I say conduct competitive analysis, I hope you took into consideration that guy, because it is he who has the ability to put you out of business faster than any recession or economic crisis.

This is a point that many books and entertainment retailers fail to realise until they find themselves in trouble.

Online retailers such as Amazon and eBay have completely wiped out certain retail categories, and iTunes has further compounded the misery of entertainment retailers.

The reason the books and entertainment retail categories are affected by online retailing is they continue to view their competition as each other.

They do not take notice of the new dynamic in the industry until it was late.

As you decide on the best media through which to channel your marketing message, it is important that you take into account the new dynamic in the retail industry.

Many people are under the illusion that marketing has become cheap because of the internet.

I hate to be the one breaking this news to you, but marketing is even more expensive than it has ever been.

The main reason for this is the lowering of the barrier to entry. While the internet has created opportunity for more people than ever to establish their own retail businesses, it has also made it difficult to reach customers.

Remember, I said you are now competing with a business run by a guy in the village in China or India; someone placing an order for product on the internet might have no idea it is being shipped from China.

This guy in the back of his car on his iPad can compete with any retailer no matter their size. Further, because of the new marketing media, consumers are overwhelmed with marketing messages that bombard them from all directions.

The average person is exposed to over three thousand advertising messages a day and that continues to increase. This does not even include popup banners and ads on social media.

Therefore, people are doing their best to avoid any message that smells like an ad. It is for this that instead of the internet making it less expensive to reach people, it is more expensive.

It does not matter what media you choose to use, online or offline, the cost of reaching prospects is skyrocketing.

Even with the skyrocketing cost, there is no guarantee that because you spend a fortune on your ad, you will reach your target audience.

In the first instance, as I pointed out early, they are already overwhelmed with advertising messages coming at them from different directions.

Secondly, you will think that with iPhones and iPads it will be easy, as people will have more spare time.

What the iPhones, iPads, social media and all the other gadgets have done, is take away peoples' ability and desire to concentrate on a single thing for a sustained period.

What your marketing message is competing with, is someone filming himself while drinking a gallon of vodka in one go; free porn and women with big boobs freely available on YouTube.

If your target audience is a young lawyer or doctor who is working a twelve-hour shift a day, what do you think will interest him after twelve hours of work? Watching girl with boobs on YouTube or reading your sales letter?

That's for you to decide.

All I am telling you is we are now living in the attention deficit age where a lot of different things vie for attention of your target audience. This is why if you want to be able to get through to them, you need to strategize.

You need to ensure you follow the process as outlined above:

- Identify you're the target market you are selling to
- Craft the right marketing message to grab their attention as they walk pass your store.-
- Select the right media through which you are going to channel the marketing message – how you are going to reach them

Challenges Facing Your Marketing Message

The first challenge you face when you send out a marketing message is, will it to be opened? Most people have spam guard to filter their emails.

If your message manages to survive the spam filter, the second challenge is, is it enticing enough to get your prospect to open it?

This is where most of the stuff we have discussed in the previous sections comes into play.

To get someone to open an email from you, your subject line has to be captivating…your message absorbing.

You will be unable to write a captivating subject line that speaks to your target market if you do not understand their thought process or know who they are.

If by some luck of the draw, you manage to pass challenge number two – he opens the email; your headline had better be able to captivate his attention in a few seconds.

Trust me, he is not going to sit there get a coffee and start reading your email; he is going to scan. Therefore, you need to ensure your email is well written and structured to stop him in his tracks and force him to read it.

By the way, a similar process applies to postal mail.

Legendary copywriter Gary Halbert once said people sort their mail over the wastebasket.

Anything that has the slightest resemblance to an ad goes into the basket.

The rest of the mail is sorted into 'A' and 'B' piles.

The 'A' pile is the important mails and the 'B' pile are the not so important mail.

Mail in the 'B' pile are the…'these look interesting, I will check them later'.

If you are lucky, at the end of the night or in the weekend, they might check the 'B' pile, in which case they might…I said might read your mail.

Therefore if you want your message to go pass the spam filter or be included in the 'A' pile, you need to ensure your marketing message does not look or smell like an ad.

So the question now, is how do you prevent your ad from looking like an ad?

I need you to listen to this answer very carefully because this is a very critical point in your marketing.

If your ad is not open or read, it does not matter how good the message is and it does not matter if it is the right target audience; it will not be acted on, which is why it is very crucial you listen to this point.

In order to ensure your ad does not end up in the wastebasket, you need to make it valuable.

What do I mean by that?

Let me explain what I mean by making your ad to look valuable.

It needs to look like something that will give not take, something away from them.

Your ad needs to look like it is something that will give them valuable information when they read it.

Your ad should not read sales all over it.

I will stick to offline media for now, but we will address a similar thing when we deal with online media.

When you want to send out an ad, you need to pay careful attention to the format it will be sent in.

If you are sending out an envelope, you need to ensure the envelope itself looks valuable.

There are certain envelopes you send a letter in that will be opened and there are envelopes you use that will end up in the wastebasket.

This comes down to the technique of addressing the envelope and stuff which we are not going to be addressing in this training.

However, understand that if you do not want your marketing message ending up in the wastebasket, you need to ensure it appears valuable.

Another way of preventing your message from ending up in the wastebasket is to send it special delivery.

This brings up another dimension in your marketing, which is to know the value to you of each customer.

Many businesses ignore the importance of knowing their numbers but knowing your numbers is the root of success of any business.

There is no way a business will become profitable if top management do not know certain numbers.

Two of the more important numbers are: the cost of your customer acquisition and the value of each customer to your business.

One reason knowing the value of each customer is important is, it will allow you to determine the amount you are willing to spend to acquire customers.

Let me stress this point, and if there is just one thing you get from this entire workbook, let it be this; *sales and marketing are buying customers.*

Do not delude yourself that you are going to build a business empire (for) free.

I always have this discussion with business owners when they come to me for help with their marketing.

A typical consultation day starts like this:

Me: Where do you want to be twelve months from now?

They will explain to me about the feelings they will like to have.

Me: 'I need figures'. I know money is not the only output but we need something we can count.

After squeezing them for a few minutes, they will come up with some random figure.

Me: How much resource do you have at your disposal to achieve that figure?

They: Most of the times it is zip…nada…zero…

I remember having a conversation with someone who told me she wanted to make a quarter of a million in twelve months.

I asked; do you know that in order to make a quarter of a million you will need a marketing budget of at least fifty thousand?

She gasped!

What is your current internal infrastructure?

What is your current skill level?

How many 'A' level talent do you currently have in your organisation?

It is impossible for an under a hundred thousand business, to move to a quarter of a million operation without adequate resources.

The main reason the majority of businesses fail is they run out of cash.

Motivational gurus, coaches and some business consultants talk about passion and belief.

It's good to be passionate about what you are doing, it's good to believe in yourself but it's also good to have the ability to take the necessary actions to achieve your goal.

Except you developed some type of whiz bag software or app, there is no way anyone is going to mathematically move a business from twenty thousand pound to a quarter of a million pounds in a year without a major cash injection.

It will never happen.

I know I have strayed from the topic, but I wanted you to get this point. *Marketing is about buying customers, if you do not have the ability or the willingness to buy customers, you might as well stop reading this workbook because it is not going to help you.*

The large majority of business owners do not want to spend a red penny on marketing or many want to spend the least amount possible on their marketing.

Here is another thing you want to write down:

Ideally, what you want to do is, put yourself in a position in which you are able to spend more on marketing than your competitors.

That should be your goal with your marketing, to put yourself in the position where you are capable of spending ten times as much on your marketing as that of your closet competitor.

The reason why companies like Nike, Coca Cola or McDonald remain the leader in their field even though they are constantly facing steep competition is, they are willing and capable of outspending all of their competitors combine more than a thousand times.

Pepsi have been trying for years to compete with coke, they have still not been able to scratch the surface of the coke market share because coke is willing and capable of outspending Pepsi by billions.

Can you imagine the amount of sportswear companies that have been trying hard to steal market share from Nike? Have they even been able to get anywhere close to Nike?

Nike is outspending all of them combined by billions.

I am not suggesting you need to spend billions on your marketing to be able to compete.

What I am suggesting is you understand that you are not going to build your retail business for, free.

You will have to deploy some resources if you want to achieve your goals or you will remain in the same position you are in currently, and someday when another person who is willing to spend on their marketing enters your niche, you will be history.

The reason I have gone off on the tantrum is just to make the point that there are times when you will have to pay for priority or special delivery in order to ensure your message is read.

It cannot be read if it is not opened, so you need to give yourself the chance of it been open.

No one, absolutely no one ever throws out FedEx, DHL or UPS.

Can you imagine someone receiving a FedEx, DHL or UPS parcel and tossing it in the waste-basket? It will never happen.

This is why knowing the value of your customer is very important.

One of the reasons for this is, posting out your marketing message with FedEx, DHL or UPS is a very expensive exercise.

However, high-end retailers, like Harrods, Harvey Nichols or Selfridges, can afford to FedEx their sales messages because they know the value of their customers.

For example if those retailers sent out hundred DHL packages, chances are two customers responding to it will get them to breakeven point and any other response will be profit.

However, if tier two or tier three retailers were to use the special delivery route, they are more likely to operate at a loss.

This is why it is important to know your numbers.

When you know the value of each customer to you, it's easy to determine the amount you are willing to spend to acquire them.

Step Two

The next step in the process is what happens when they open the envelope.

Just like the email, you have only a few seconds to capture their attention.

Paying for special delivery does not mean that your message is will be read.

The 'special delivery' only ensures it is opened.

Once it is open, you need to give the recipient a reason to read it.

Again, they will only read it if it provides value to them.

Let me use our own marketing strategy as an illustration.

Our core product is consulting.

However, we have series of other products.

We have a home study course called 'How to Increase Retail Sales'.

We have a book called 'How to Increase Retail Sales'.

And we have leaflets that we use to promote the various products.

If we wanted to attract a retail client, which one of the three will we use?

The answer is it depends.

If we wanted to attract Harrods, Marks & Spencer, Next or John Lewis we are not going to send their CEO the book or leaflet.

We will send them the home study course plus the book.

And we will send them by special delivery because we know any of those accounts could land us hundreds of thousands.

However, if we were to send our marketing information to a smaller retailer, again depending on how valuable we perceive them to be, we will send the home study course or the book.

We will only use the leaflet in circumstances where we have no chance of accessing the prospect and we only wanted to leave information.

Example if I attended a retail event, and I had no means of talking with many of the decision makers at the event, I will locate my leaflet at strategic locations of the venue where I was convinced they will be seen.

But here is the point.

If I wanted to pass the open test with a retailer, I will send the book or home study course by special delivery.

There is no retailer in this world who will open an envelope, sees a book or home study course that says 'how to increase retail sales', who will throw it away.

It will never happen; they will at least check it out.

The point I am trying to make here is, by providing them valuable information up front, it ensure that:

- One: my marketing material is opened
- Two: It is read

My book and home study course are used as our marketing materials.

Step Three

The third step in the process is the follow-up sequence.

You cannot be so arrogant to think that the moment they receive your marketing material, because it is valuable they will drop everything and read it.

To think in that manner is naive. As I said previously, people are busy; they have work to do and family to attend to.

Therefore, it is quite possible that a few minutes after they receive your message, they would have already forgotten about it.

The euphoria of receiving a parcel will wear off after ten minutes and they will be back to where they were.

Secondly, even if they read your message, they might not have a need for your product or service at that time. They might not be able to afford it, they might have another supplier or their brother-in-law might be their present vendor and they will not want to upset him.

Many other things might prevent them from acting on your offer at that point even though they found it very valuable. This is why the follow-up process is very important. Getting qualified prospects to at least read or listen to your offer and ultimately to become customers, requires repetition.

Repetition to the masses is very expensive so it is important you market to only your target. Only then will repetition be cost effective.

When I say repetition, I am not suggesting you send out the same book or home study course multiple times although that will be the most effective way, it will be too expensive.

I am suggesting in the first instance you send something valuable; it could be sample products. If the products you are advertising are very expensive, you could send them accessories.

After you have sent the first valuable stuff, you could follow it up with more stuff that is valuable, a letter or a post card. Then you can follow it up with a phone call, then another phone call and email.

Here is the thinking behind this process: the goal is not to become a pest that just keeps sending junk in the name of follow-up.

You need to be tactical about the process and respectful of the other person.

There are four things you want to achieve in your communication with your prospects.

- You must get them to read or listen to your proposition
- You must get them to understand the benefits
- You must get them to have confidence in your organisation's ability to fulfil the promised benefit
- You must motivate them to take action

You will not achieve the above by making them angry with you. You will only achieve it by being very tactical in your communication.

You cannot send the same information to them every time; it will be classed as junk or spam.

Every time you communicate with them, the goal has to be to leave them better than they were when they received your communication.

This is one of the reasons every retailer should have a newsletter so that in a worst-case scenario, you can send out your newsletter.

But above all, your follow-up process has to be systematic, deliberate, tactical and valuable to the prospects.

Your Website

Our websites have become the principal means of delivering our marketing message.

In fact, for most retailers their website is the only means through which they deliver their marketing message.

Their store is to sell their merchandise, but their website is their only marketing tool they have.

As a said previously, for most retailers, their business is their online storefront.

There are thousands of retailers whose business as they will describe it is their website.

This section is not meant to address an ecommerce website, but brick and mortar retailers who also sell through their website and use their website to drive traffic to their store.

There are three types of websites:

- Brochure website
- e-commerce website
- Lead generation website

The common trend that runs through all three is:

- Traffic generation
- Traffic conversion

What the majority of retailers have is brochure website; they hope will work as a lead generation magnet.

Let me quickly give the difference between the three.

A brochure website as the name implies, is a brochure that only tells visitors about you and your business.

This is usually the type of website favoured by big retailers.

Many of them are now changing their websites to an e-commerce site.

A brochure site contains information about the organisation.

However, many small and independent retailers have adopted the corporate look on their websites without understanding the reason large retail organisations have a brochure website.

The second type of website is an e-website. The goal of an ecommerce website is basically to be used as an online store.

The lead generation website, which as the name implies is for generating leads is the one most retailers ought to have.

In fact, every business needs to have a lead generation website even if it had a brochure website to satisfy the guys in the head office.

A lead generation website has a single goal that is to attract leads that later become customers.

Ninety-nine percent of retailers with a website are not achieving the goal for which they built their websites.

There are two reasons for this.

Firstly, many retailers do not construct their websites with any set objective; they just wanted to have a website.

Secondly, many retailers do not even know that their websites need to be constructed with a specific objective.

Many retailers have their website designed by designers who know nothing about marketing.

Those designers know about design but they do not know marketing, therefore do not build the site with the objective of attracting customers.

Your website has to be incorporated into your overall marketing scheme; this means it needs to be functional.

At the beginning, I spoke about my Bulgarian friend who is an architect.

When he draws a building, he draws the building the way it is expected to look when it is occupied.

I asked why he designed his buildings that way; he said architecture these days is about functionality.

The building is being constructed for a specific reason. It is either a residential or commercial premises.

The purpose for which the building is constructed has to be taken into account.

The building has to be made to suit the needs of the occupants not the other way round.

The same principle has to be applied to your website.

You need to construct your website to take into account the reason for which it is been constructed.

Since it is obvious that the majority of retailers construct their website to generate leads, it goes without saying that the website has to be made in a specific way to facilitate the generation of leads.

Your website as a lead generation magnet needs to focus on two things:

- A good marketing message that speaks directly to you target audience
- Functionality

Don't panic I am not going to go all technical on you, my goal in this section is to provide you the fundamentals of your website design, so that when you speak to your technical person you will know the questions to ask them and the results to expect.

When it comes to your website, the key phrase you always need to keep at the top of your mind is *user experience*.

What is the user experience of your website?

Just think about it this way.

When someone enters your store, you expect them to find the things they are looking for, easily right?

If they have to struggle to find what they are looking for, do you think they will remain in the store or will ever return?

A Similar principle applies to your website.

When someone visits your website, they are there for a particular reason, if they cannot easily find what they are looking for, they will leave.

You do not get to have a second chance.

You need to be able to answer the following three questions about your website:

- Who am I trying to persuade?
- What action do I want them to take?
- What action do they want to take?

You can see from the first question, that it boils down to what we have been speaking about all through this workbook, your marketing message and your target market.

When you arrive at my website, there is no doubt that, my target market is small to medium size business owners. It is written there in black and white.

But it is also speaking to a specific type of small business owner, the one who wants more customers, who needs a business and marketing plan.

It is also evident what I like them to do, fill in my opt-in form. And I capture their details.

As a reward for giving me their details, they receive a business growth report. Plus they can sign up for a free business growth and marketing consultation.

On all of my lead generation landing pages, you will observe that I follow the similar pattern:

- This is what I have

- This is what it will do for you
- This is why I am doing it
- This is what I'd like you to do

Another element of your website you need to pay attention to is *functionality and user experience*.

There is a big difference between functionality and user experience.

Functionality: does your website do what it was constructed for? I.e. capture leads, sell products or sell your services.

User experience: can users easily find what they are looking for? Again, this is a very crucial point:

There is what you want the website to do.

There is what the user wants to do for coming to your website.

There is a thin line between your desire and the user's desire.

The genius comes from your ability to merge your wants with your user needs.

Conversion

This brings us to the second critical aspect of any website – conversion.

I have somewhat discussed the elements of conversion when speaking about functionality, usability and customer experience.

Conversion is simply getting visitors to take the action you like them to take when they arrive on your site.

To get them to take the actions you want them to take, your marketing message has to appeal to them and the website has to be designed to make it easy for them to take the action you would like them to take.

What I really want to talk about in terms of conversion now is the structure of your sales funnel.

Your Sales Funnel

Your sales funnel is your customer buying process, the steps they need to go through to buy from you.

There is the marketing funnel, which is the steps required for getting them into your store.

The marketing funnel is the process we have been discussing up until this point:

- Identifying your target audience
- Crafting an effective marketing message
- Selecting the right media through which to channel your marketing message
- Your website
- Your follow up sequence

The sales funnel is what happens once they are in the store.

This goes back to the discussion about customer experience.

What happens when someone enters your store?

How are they greeted at the entrance?

Can they easily locate merchandise in your store?

If they need assistance, is it readily available?

Are your store assistants capable of answering their questions?

I previously told stories of my experience with four retailers:

- Harrods
- Richer Sound
- Next
- PC World

At Harrods, there are store assistants stood at every corner of the store within a few meters from every customer.

Richer Sound continues to break records for the highest sales per square foot because they have the most knowledgeable retail staff in the entire UK.

I was at Next to shop with my son, I could not find what I was looking for, I stood for over fifteen minutes trying to find a store assistant to ask, I could not find one so I left. And this did not happen in one Next store, it happened in two.

Like Next, when I went to PC World, I stood at the checkout waiting to pay, while a few meters from me staff members chatted about the Manchester derby. On many occasions, the security officer had to serve customers.

As you can see, there are very different sales processes from each of these retailers that create completely different experience for customers.

What I am saying to you here is; your sales process needs to be systematised.

From the moment someone enters your store until the time they leave, everything needs to be systematised.

You do not increase your sales by having a sales process that is haphazard.

The same thing needs to apply to your website.

When someone pays for products on your website, how easy it is for them to receive confirmation of purchase?

The biggest barrier to sales whether online or offline, is trust.

First, many people have been burned by legitimate businesses that do not keep their promise. Customer service is at an all-time low. Therefore, consumers level of scepticism is higher than it used to be years ago.

People are even more sceptical when buying over the internet.

So the question you need to answer through your website presentation and marketing message is this: *have you made an effort through your website design, presentation and message to increase credibility and decrease scepticism?*

The more credible your website appears in terms of your message and presentation, the easier it will be for customers to do business with you.

Trust is absolutely necessary when selling online.

The second thing is, how easy is it for them to receive their purchase.

When you promise a delivery date, do you ensure the product arrives on that date?

Thirdly, what is your after sales process?

What happens after they have bought?

Do you get in touch with them to find out if they are satisfied with their purchase?

Do you even call to check whether they have received their purchase or?

Or do you expect them to call screaming if they have not?

It might cost you a few hundreds per month to get someone contacting your customers after the sale to ensure they have received their purchase.

But that could make the difference between the person purchasing from you another time and them not buying from you again.

Website Conversion

The most neglected aspect of using your website as an effective marketing tool is conversion.

In an ideal situation, this part of the process would have been the second step in the process because we:

- Construct a website
- Drive traffic to it
- Convert the traffic

However, when discussing website I like to do it the other way round…

- First construct the website
- Put in mechanism for conversion
- Then drive traffic

The first thing I will say about conversion is this: Never, never underestimate the difficulty of getting someone to put their hands in their wallet and give you their money whether you are selling on the internet or face-to-face.

As a retailer, you are aware of the fact that the majority of times, the sale process collapses at the point of sale because this is where people begin to have a second thought.

If you are selling bread, sugar or milk and you are the only off license in town, then you need not worry about conversion.

However, if you are in any other retail category, know that it is extremely difficult to get another human being to part with their money.

The reason many retailers lose sales at this point is they underestimate the difficulties of this part of the sales process, therefore do not give it the level of seriousness it requires.

In this instant, we are dealing with conversion in the context of your website.

However, it is important that you understand that you need a good conversion process in every spectrum of your business *whether it's on the web or during face-to-face transaction.*

When someone enters your retail store, getting them to enter the store is one-step in the sales process.

Getting them to actually remove their wallet and pay for your merchandise is the most difficult step in the process, which is why we are focusing on store design and visual merchandising display.

These are few of the things, which result in a good customer experience.

What I am about to teach you is very powerful stuff so I must caution you not to use it for evil because you will end up in business hell.

I am not about to teach you trickery or underhand tactics used by unscrupulous sale people to persuade people to make decisions that is not in their best interest.

It is about genuinely holding your target audience hands and helping them make a decision that is in their best interest not decisions that are bad for them but you persuade them to take it simply because you want to make quick profit out of them.

You will not get rich like that and I promise you, you will end up in business hell if you use this information for evil.

Conversion is what has made Amazon the most dominant retailer in the world today.

Online retailers like Amazon and eBay have hundreds of staff sat in their office watching the activities of every single visitor to their sites.

Based upon the data they receive, they keep changing their site design to suit their visitors in order to increase their conversion rate.

Recently, when I attended the retail technology exhibition, one of the most popular gadgets on display was the customer tracking technologies.

These are technologies that can be used to track the activities of customers in your store, in real time.

These are the types of technologies being used by the most successful retailers because they understand the benefit of knowing their customers. They know customer knowledge is the most effective way of increasing conversion.

The first critical point about conversion that I need you to know is; never design your sales and marketing funnel around your technology, it needs to be the other way around.

You need to design your conversion technology around your sales and marketing funnel.

What you have with most small and medium size retail organisations is they will hire tech guys to create systems for them.

The techies will create systems that the retailers lack the technical knowledge or the resources to use effectively. So whatever system you decide to design has to account for your current resources and technical capabilities within your organisation.

The second critical point you need to take into consideration is the length of your sales funnel will depend on the extent of beliefs you need to establish in your target audience before they buy and into the cost of the products on offer.

The more expensive your merchandise are, the further removed your target audience is from your brand, the more steps you need to include in your sales funnel to convince them.

When we go into the section about traffic generation, I will expand on the sequence of events required to drive traffic to your website, however, I briefly touch on the traffic generation process here to illustrate this point even better.

Let's say you bought traffic from google ad. Someone clicks on your ad on google; it takes them to your website. Clicking on the ad is the first step in your sales process.

When they land on your website, the action you want them to take is the second step in the process.

When they land on your website, you have your merchandise on display, the decision as to whether they will buy will depend on several factors:

- The trust they have for your brand
- The way the product is presented
- The description of the products on the site
- The ease of purchase

That is what conversion is all about.

> *You need to ensure your website design looks like a business that can be trusted. Your merchandise are presented in eye catching manner, the description of the merchandise is clear and that they can easily purchase what they like and leave the site.*

Conversion is about the little things that can make the difference. You need to have the ability to test and monitor the activities of visitors to your site.

The reason most websites never convert traffic is, once they build their website, it is fait accompli, they never make any type of changes to it.

Your website need to dynamic, it cannot be static.

Think of the last time you made any type of changes to your website.

I am sure you will admit you have never touched your website since the time the designer gave it to you.

Do you not clean your store?

Has it not been cleaned since you moved into it?

Your website is like your store, it needs constant cleaning if you want it to serve the purpose for which it was built.

Traffic Generation

Basically, this should have been the second step in the process of your website design.

I left it until the last deliberately because what I am going to speak about with regard to traffic goes totally against what many of you have been taught or told about traffic generation.

There are two ways for driving traffic to your website:

- Free traffic
- Paid traffic

Free traffic is traffic as the word implies is you can get free to your website.

It is traffic from social media, blogs, forums, articles directories or links from other sites.

Paid traffic is what you get from Google, Bing, other search engines and social media sites.

Getting free traffic requires lots of search engine optimisation (SEO) i.e. using keywords on your website, posting contents on social media, article directories, forums, blogs and directories.

The majority of small to medium size retailers build their websites and never attempt to drive traffic to it in any form whatever.

They believe that the fact that they have a website someone searching online will stumble on it.

The few who are smart enough to know that they need traffic, focus most of their attention of free traffic.

Let me drop the bombshell.

The concept of free traffic is a myth. Yes, I said the concept of free traffic is a myth. There is nothing like free traffic.

Free is those phrases used by smart internet marketers to extract money from people who like freebies. It's like paying to sleep in a homeless shelter or buying food at the food bank.

The reason it is called homeless shelter you are expected to be given free shelter for the night without having to cough up money from your pocket.

The same applies to the food bank.

Because those services are for people you cannot afford to pay for them, they are not only free, but they are located in areas that are easily accessible to people who need them.

Contrast that to so-called free traffic.

Doing proper SEO for a website to remotely have a chance of appearing on the first page of google, not even the first spot will take a minimum of three to six months.

That is for your website to have the remotest chance of showing up in a google search.

Imagine you are a small to medium size retailers trying to drive traffic to your website. You have to post on social media, forums, blog, article directories, and all the rest; do you know how much time that will take you?

If you cannot afford to do it yourself, which is the case with many small to medium size retailers, you have to pay someone to do it.

So if you have to pay for it each month, is the traffic free?

The majority of retailers on the first page of google are either insignificant retailers that have got there by default because their websites have been up and running for a long time or they pay for the privilege.

So if there is no free traffic, what will I advise a small to medium size retailer to do if they want to generate traffic to their website?

I will advise you buy paid traffic in the first instant.

You can use a mixture of both, free as people will describe it and paid traffic.

However, if you want customers to come to your store like yesterday and you are hoping that you will attract customers to your store by posting on social media, forums or article directories; I offer my condolences.

Social Media

Last week as I was writing this workbook, the Turkish government shut down Twitter and YouTube.

Social media was widely credited with fuelling the Arab Spring that removed Arab strongmen who had been in power for years.

The election of President Barack Obama was widely attributed to his campaign team's effective use of social media.

Social media has also been responsible for some negative things like the London riot, binge drinking and bullying.

As a result of many of the above incidences, social media is now viewed by most businesses as an effective marketing tool. It is indeed an effective marketing tool if you are prepared to pay for it.

Like the myth about a free website free, free social media for business is a myth.

Collectively the social media sites have over two billon people. Facebook alone has close to a billion people.

Therefore, there is the possibility that you will find your target audience on one or more of the social media platforms.

Effective use of social media comes down to the other fundamentals we have spoken about in the other sections, selecting the right target audience and constructing a strong marketing message.

But, this is a big but.

To imagine you are going to post stuff on social media and, build your business from it is an illusion.

I have had training from the best online marketers in the world. I have attended the training of at least the top twenty online marketers in the world.

Not a single one of them ever teach social media as a source of generating traffic, paid traffic yes, but not free traffic.

There is only one of them, Dan Crowther who teach social media as a source of traffic, but that is his niche. That is how he makes his money.

Like Crowther, the only people who make money for free from social media are those who teach it.

The irony is this, even those who teach social media, pay for the traffic to advertise their training. They do not just post on social media for free and expect people to attend their training.

I know of a Facebook trainer you spend thousands of dollars per month to advertise her Facebook training course in which she show people how to use Facebook for their business for free.

Can you imagine the irony in that?

She pays for her ads to teach people how to get free traffic from Facebook.

If she knows how to it free traffic from Facebook why doesn't she use those strategies herself?

I am sure when you saw social media for retailers in the table of contents, this was not what you were expecting.

You were expecting me to show you strategies for generating free social media traffic.

I am sorry if I disappointed you.

If you were running a political campaign like President Obama, or you were trying to remove your government from power, I can show you ways of using social media for free.

But there is absolutely no business, I repeat, no business that is growing their customer base as a result of free traffic from social media.

That's a myth!

If there were a way of using social media for free, the best online marketers in the world who are making hundreds of millions from the internet would have taught it to us.

Even Dan Crowther does not get free traffic from social media, by the way.

He no longer teaches social; maybe that's because he senses people are catching on.

Workshop

1. Do you conduct lead generation activities to attract customers to your store?

_____

_____

_____

2. Which lead generation activities do you engaged in?

_____

_____

_____

3. Do you have a customer conversion strategy to convert shoppers who enter your store?

_____

_____

_____

4. What customer conversion activities are you engage in?

_____

_____

_____

5. What are your strategies for triggering repeat purchase?

_____

_____

_____

6. What type of website do you have: brochure, ecommerce or lead generation website?

_____

_____

_____

7. Was your website constructed with your customers in mind? Do your website increase the level of trust visitors have when they visit it?

_____

_____

_____

8. What is your website traffic generation strategies? Do you buy traffic or do you expect to get free traffic?

_____

_____

_____

9. Is your social media activities geared towards getting free social media traffic?

_____

_____

_____

10. When was the last you redesign your website?

_____

_____

_____

Module Two:

Store Design Blueprint: How to Use Store Design to Increase Sales

In the first module, we focused on the psychology of store design and visual merchandise display...How to influence customers behaviour.

We said that the psychological aspect of the process is very essential because without getting the thought behind the process right, it is impossible to get the strategy right.

In this module, we are going to outline the actual process of designing your store to:

- Attract customers
- Retain them for longer in the store
- Persuade them to buy
- Trigger repeat custom

We are going to focus on:

- How To Increase Retail Sales With Attractive Store Design
- How to Design your Store For Increase Customer Flow
- How To Choose Your Store Colour And Layout
- The Best Retail Store Lighting System
- How To Wow Customers With Creative Storefront Design
- How To Choose The Right Materials For Store Design

Store Design for Functionality

The very first principle of a good store design is something that I touched on in the last module; design for functionality.

It is not about how beautiful the store looks, it is about how the store will appeal to shoppers as they walk pass it.

Have you ever heard the saying beauty is in the eyes of the beholder?

That is what I am talking about.

When designing your store, always think and ask yourself, will this stop or attract my target audience?

Secondly, functionality is about the ease with which your customers can navigate your store: walk through the aisles, find what they are looking for, get assistance, reach products etc.

Thirdly, how easy will it be for them to make payment and exit the store?

Fourthly, what can you put in the design to trigger automatic upsell?

These are the things your store design needs to be about.

One company that embodies the concept of functionality in its products design is Apple.

Here are three things that are great about Apple products:

- Simplicity
- Functionality
- Elegance

The daftest person could take an Apple product and in a few minutes know how to use it. This is because when apple designers sit to design their products, they ask these questions:

- Who are we designing this product for?
- What work do they do?
- Where do they live?
- How would this product make their work or personal life easier?
- What else would they be able to do with this product in the future?
- What else would they want to do with this product?
- How can this product change their life for the better?

It is only after they have answered the above questions that they decide on the product design.

A similar thought process goes into the design of cars, whether it is Mercedes-Benz, BMW or Ferrari.

Their designers ask themselves those questions prior to designing their cars.

Mercedes-Benz appeals to a completely different audience from BMW or Ferrari.

While the average Mercedes-Benz owner might focus on comfort or luxury, the BMW or Ferrari owner might focus on speed.

Therefore, as the designers of these automobile manufacturers sit to design their cars, they concentrate on fulfilling the desires of their target audience.

Google arguably one of the most successful businesses of our time has the same web page that it had since it started.

Even though they 'Googlies' their logo every day, the design of the webpage remains the same.

Retail store design like any other design is subject to similar design principles.

In order for a retail store to achieve similar phenomenal success as any other successful business, retail stores have to conform to the same fundamental design principles that make other businesses successful.

I once watched an interview with a Ferrari executive. He said when you drive a Ferrari, you drive a dream.

Look at your current store design and ask yourself the following questions:

- Was it designed with the customer in mind?
- Does it fit with your customers' avatar?
- Did you take into account your competition?
- Is your store design simple, functional and clear?
- Does your store design represent your core message?

Design your store for easy customer flow

Harrods is one of the most successful retailers in the world.

One of the things that make Harrods so successful is its store design.

For example when parents visit Harrods children department with their kids, there is open space for the kids to play.

They even have play consultants to play with the kids.

Think about this and imagine a kid playing with a particular toy in Harrods with a play consultant; the consultant throws the ball to the kid, the kid throws the ball back; soon the kid is laughing and enjoying the game.

Do you think that at the end of the game the kid will want to leave the store without the ball?

Contrast this with Early Learning Centre or Toys R Us. These stores sell children's' stuff to. However, they are like a Soviet Dental suite.

Do you think the kids or their parents will have good buying experience in those stores?

I think not.

When we talk about store design functionality, this is what designing for functionality means.

Harrods creates the atmosphere in its store to get parent and children in a buying mood while Early Learning Centre or Toys R Us creates the atmosphere that results in discomfort for both parent and kids, thereby reducing their desire to buy.

Your store design has to:

- Attract customers as they pass by the store
- Entice them to enter the store
- Retain them longer in the store
- Persuade them to buy

Not one of these four core elements would stand out as a single factor that on its own can result in increased sales.

However, if it is a case of being forced to choose one from four, I will say retaining customers in the store would be the most important of the four.

This is because the longer customers stay in the store; the more likely they are to buy.

To hold customers in your store for a long time, they need to be able to move freely within the store without any form of hindrance.

A retail store has three basic design components:

- Selling area
- Service area
- Circulation area

The extent to which these areas are effectively utilised, especially the selling area is the extent to which you will succeed in placing your customers in a buying mood.

Shopping is a favoured pastime for many people. For a great many people shopping is a necessity.

However, recreational shopping is more prevalent than shopping out of necessity.

Visit any city centre at the weekend and you will notice the High Street jam-packed with shoppers.

Despite the hoard of people in the city centre, as you walk around, you will notice some stores are jammed packed while some stores are empty.

The reason for this is, for most people the act of going shopping is an event.

Those who buy for recreational purposes do not go shopping just to buy things; they love the experience of going to shopping. For them, it's a day out.

21st century retailing is not about buying and selling, it is also about the experience that customers have in the process. It is about the atmosphere in the store and the comfort customers feel in the store.

Starbucks sells coffee like many other coffee shops, yet people prefer Starbucks to other coffee shops.

Starbucks does not sell some types of technologically advanced coffee that is proven to give long life, yet customers prefer Starbucks over other Cafes.

This is due to the fact that Starbucks creates an environment in which customers feel relaxed and comfortable.

When customers feel this way they are more inclined to purchase from you.

An Apple store in a shopping centre is always full of people. Even in the middle of the day when most retail stores are empty, Apple stores are always buzzing with people.

The reason for that is Apple stores are cool places to be.

Furthermore, there is no queuing for payment at the checkout counter in an Apple store. All the sales assistants carry a payment device.

Good advertising and promotion works to bring customers into your store.

However, when they are in the store, their decision to buy could be down to the layout and design.

Both play a huge role in how customers rate their experiences, whether they buy and if they return or recommend your store to their family and friends.

What is customer flow?

Customer flow in a retail environment refers to the manner in which customers move from the point of entry into the store until they leave the store.

Customer flow refers to:

- The ease with which customers walk through the aisles
- The ease with which they gain access to merchandise to sample products or choose
- The speed with which their questions are answered
- The ease with which they pay for merchandise and exit the store

A good customer flow system should respond to customer's choice.

The customer should have visible options. These ought to include easy access to products and customer service that results in a positive impression of your store.

In a retail environment where the entire operation depends on various actors and factors, customer flow doesn't just happen. It must be purposely created as a part of your store design blueprint, managed and continuously improved to take into account the changing retail environment.

Aisle signage and shelf labelling form part of your customer flow system.

Throughout the store signage and labelling should be set to enable customers locate merchandise easily and familiarise themselves with the store layout.

What are the various types of store design?

Listed below are the three basic types of store designs that encourage customer flow:

Free flow design

A free flow design system allows products to be arranged throughout the store.

A free flow store design is used mainly boutiques, clothing, jewellery, and specialty stores.

Grid pattern design

Mostly drugstores, supermarkets and superstores use a Grid pattern design.

Spine design

The spine design contains elements of the free flow and the grid pattern design.

With the spine design, merchandise is displayed on both sides of the aisle using either the free flow or grid layout or a combination of the two.

How to use store design to increase customer flow

A research into customer flow in the UK revealed that 75% of customers only see a maximum of 25% of merchandise on display in retail stores.

Pause and think for a moment! What will happen to your sales if your customers see at a glance, all of the products on display in your store?

Or if it was the other way round, if your customers see 75% of the merchandise in your store?

This is what the objective of your design store needs to be. You need to design your store in such a way that it forces your customers to walk around the entire store.

Furthermore, the aim has to be to create a design that ensures you deliberately directed customers around the store, instead of leaving them to walk aimlessly around the store.

The following are ways of designing your store to force the movement of customers around it:

Positioning your checkout counters

The position of your checkout counters is critical for controlling the movement of customers in your store.

Generally, customers walk away from checkout counters because checkout counters remind them that they are going to spend money.

Therefore, it is crucial that you position the checkout counter in such a way that it is not the first thing customers see when they enter the store.

After they are relaxed, they will naturally gravitate towards it.

The right positioning of your checkout counter can result in increased sales.

Control customer movement

You are designing to encourage customer movement around the store.

To achieve this, merchandise needs to be strategically displayed to encourage shoppers to move from one end of the store to the next and in the process view other merchandise.

The way to ensure this is to place essential products in different locations of the store.

Especially essential products such as:

- Milk
- Bread
- Sugar
- Toilet paper
- Detergent
- Coffee
- Beverages

Strategically locating this merchandise around your store will force customers to walk around in search of them.

Make adequate use of sightlines

Sightlines are a very critical component for encouraging customer flow.

They attract customer's attention as they move around the store and they generate curiosity.

Strategically locating sightlines in your store would encourage customers to move around and get to know what products on display.

Create destination departments

There needs to be destination departments in key locations of your store and ensure customers are aware of them. They need to be strategically located close to the entrance and exit points and in high traffic areas of the store.

Examples of such departments may be:

- The Power Tool Department
- The Seedling or Bedding Plants department
- The Ski Department
- The In-house Deli
- Lighting
- Shoe
- Electronics
- Technology

Use the right lighting system

At all times, your customers need to be able to see easily, as they walk around the store. Product areas need to be properly lit to attract their attention. When customers feel trapped or lost in your store they will promptly leave.

Create narrow aisles

Create narrow aisle space that would slow down customers as they walk around your store and get them to look at more products. However, the aisles have to be wide enough for the comfort of the customer. Wide aisle space encourages customers to move fast through them without actually browsing the products especially if they already know what they want to buy.

Strategically locate high demand products

High demand merchandise needs to be located at the end of the aisles.

This encourages customers to walk pass other products before getting to them.

Display impulse items strategically

Display impulse buys, small and constantly in need and regularly purchased products close to checkout counter and in high traffic areas.

Strategically locate promotional products

Feature or promotional products should never be placed at the entrance to your store. When customers enter your store, they need time to adjust to the environment. They are less likely to pay careful attention to products that they see as they enter.

Do not neglect disabled customers

When designing your store, consideration has to be made for customers with disabilities and special needs. Aisles need to be wide enough to accommodate wheelchairs or a mother with a pram.

A successful store design strategy creates a store that leaves your customers with a happy experience. However, it is essential that you regularly refresh your design to take into account and reflect changing trends.

How to Choose Your Store Colour and Layout

The appearance of a store is often fundamental to the success of that store.

The most successful retailers maintain a consistent layout, colour scheme and other thematic elements that help customers recognise the organisation.

The colour and layout of a retail store can be the difference between a great shopping experience and one that results in a shopper exiting your store empty-handed.

A good store layout will not only help you influence customer's behaviour; by properly designing customer flow, merchandise placement and the entire ambiance; it also provides you with an understanding of sales per square foot.

This can help you properly determine the extent to which you are utilising your selling space.

Below is a breakdown of the benefits of having good store layout:

Good layout enhance store image:
Having the right layout can enhance your overall image.

Predict customer buying behaviour

The strategic arrangement of fixtures, strategic placement of staircases, escalators and departments affect store traffic and the amount of time customers spend in your store.

Maximize selling space

You can measure the productivity of your sales space per square foot by monitoring the sales figure of each area in your store.

Implement contextual display

The implementation of a contextual display is another way of making effective use of your display space. Merchandise that are somewhat related can be displayed in the same location. This is likely to trigger impulse buying and maximise the use of your selling space.

Use layout to instigate positive emotions

Your store layout can determine the customers' emotion and sentiment they display while they are in your store.

The emotions your store layout triggers in customers as they walk around would determine whether they buy or not.

Loss prevention

In the final analysis, your ultimate desire is to make a profit. The best way of making profit is to increase sales and reduce shrinkage. Creative arrangement of your merchandise, fixtures and layout can reduce the possibility of crime in your store.

The importance of colour in store design

Colour is a very critical aspect of your store design.

Colour is a very powerful intangible aspect of a design that if used properly can result in enormous benefit for the store.

On the other hand executed poorly, it can result in loss sales. Colour has a huge effect on the mood of people.

Colour can stimulate happiness, relaxation; a feeling of comfort or, it can result in anxiety and restlessness.

Consequently, as you make the decision on the colour of your store, the deciding factor has to be what emotion you want to trigger in your customers.

Choosing a colour scheme to distinguish your store from the competition is somewhat of an art and a science, and it depends on your type of store and the image you wish to convey.

There are a lot of guidelines regarding colour application.

For instance, dark colour is inappropriate for small spaces. Painting a space white makes it appear larger and grander. Colours such as blue, purple, white and green are believed to encourage a feeling of calm and relaxation.

It is believed that stores decorated with these colours stimulate a feeling of rationalisation and positive thoughts in the minds of customers, resulting in them spending more in those stores.

Customers in stores with those colours are generally calmer, go about their shopping slowly and stay longer in the store.

On the other hand, stores with red or orange considered hot colours, generate a feeling of anxiety and claustrophobia in their customers.

Customers in those stores do not stay long because they feel uneasy, restless and impatient.

However, all colours have their pros and cons. Bright colours such as red and orange are excellent colours for attracting attention to your store. In most instances, the first thing a customer notices when on a shopping spree is not the name of the retailer or its brand logo but its colour.

The Best Retail Store Lighting System

The quality of light in your store is a very significant determinant of the success of your store.

> Good lighting is important for:
> - Attracting customers into your store
> - Guiding them through the store
> - Helping them evaluate the products
> - Helping your store associates to complete a sale swiftly and accurately

In addition to the above light is closely linked to:

> - Increasing store sales
> - Providing customers with a good impression of your store
> - Increasing the perceived value of your products
> - Creating a conducive shopping environment for your customers

The most common things taken into consideration whenever retailers think of ways of increasing sales are:

> - Increased advertising
> - Intensive promotion
> - New product lines
> - Changing store fixtures
> - Relocating products

The lighting scheme of their store is never taken into consideration. But a good quality lighting system in your store enhances the look of both the store and the display.

When your store appearance is enhanced because of good lighting, customers are more likely to believe that the products in your store are of high quality. The core of marketing is perception…what the customer thinks about your store.

Attracting customers into your store

The style of lighting you have in your store should signal to your customers that your store is open for business.

Your lighting system needs to breed curiosity in shoppers as they pass by your store.

Guide them through the store

You lighting needs to guide customers around the store and to specific areas you would like them to see.

When you make effective use of accent lighting, you can control customers' movement within the store and persuade them to go from one department to the next if only to see what's on display.

Helping customers evaluate the products

An adequately lit area makes it easier for customers to weigh up merchandise and make buying decisions.

When customers have the opportunity to check out products without any form of hindrance, they are more likely to make a buying decision.

Helping your store associates complete sale swiftly and accurately

The point-of-sale, customer service desk, changing rooms and all other points of the store where store associates are expected to serve customers, need to be well lit so they could perform their duties easily.

Listed below are the most commonly used retail lighting systems:

Ambient Lighting

Ambient lighting is the basic lighting system in a retail store that aids customers' movement around the store and helps them to evaluate products.

Accent Lighting

Accent lighting commonly known as "focus" lighting is used to draw attention to a few products in a retail store. This is particularly useful for highlighting high ticket or promotional products.

High Activity Lighting

High Activity Lighting schemes focus attention on a particular area of the store.

Shelf and Case Lighting

Shelf and Case Lighting is used in display cabinets and shelves where certain high ticket or exclusive items are displayed.

Perimeter and Valance Lighting

The Perimeter lighting scheme is used for tall vertical shelving and displays.

Architectural Lighting

The Architectural lighting scheme is best to light up and highlight the architectural design of a building.

Task Lighting

Task lights are installed specifically for use by staff assigned to specific tasks.

Below are some important factors to consider when installing lighting systems in your store:

- Colour rendering index/colour temperature
- Contrast/accent/highlight
- Daylight Integration/regulator
- Direct glare/reflected glare
- Image/style
- Modelling of objects/shadows
- Visual priority/organization
- Quantity of light on vertical displays
- Quantity of light on horizontal surfaces
- Use high colour rendering lights

When selecting your lighting system, you need to ensure that the types of bulbs you choose make product colours appear as natural as possible.

What to look for when selecting your lighting system?

The specification on the packaging that indicates it renders colours accurately.

Colour rendering index (CRI) is specified on bulb packaging or in manufacturer's catalogues.

CRI of lights ranges from one to as high as a hundred. For your store, you need to select lights with a CRI of 80 or above. Some standard halogen, incandescent, fluorescent and metal halide lights meet the 80 and above CRI value.

Lighting fixtures should limit glare

Ensure that the type of lighting system you choose limits the customer's view of the light louvers, baffles, and lenses.

Lighting system such as accent Lighting, should be aimed directly at the merchandise.

Properly distributed light

Light should be evenly distributed throughout your store.

The entrance, areas between aisles and displays have to be well lit to ensure customers are able to see merchandise properly as they move around the store.

Since most merchandise are displayed vertically, it is essential that the lighting system you select have the ability to properly light vertical surfaces.

Below is a further guide for choosing and implementing an effective lighting system:

- Place the lighting source as close as possible to the merchandise.
- For ambient lighting, use efficient diffusers such as fluorescents.
- For accent lighting, use narrow beam spotlights such as Halogen PARs or Low-Voltage MR-16s.
- Brighten up your store aisles with spill light from the accented merchandising areas or displays.
- Use the lightest colours on the interior surfaces of shelving.
- Ensure you use organized patterns of lighting fixtures. Chaotic patterns may confuse, agitate or fatigue the customers.
- Ensure you use high colour rendering lamps for both ambient and task lighting
- In clothing stores, the lights must be adequate in sales areas and dressing rooms so that customers can see how the items look prior to purchasing.

While lighting must attract customers to your store, the objective needs to be to enable customers to read signage and move unhindered throughout the store.

The level and quality of the illumination in your store will create a lasting impression on your customers and will be the key to whether customers buy or return to your store.

Be aware that the lighting system is as dynamic as the products you display; therefore you cannot be rigid about it.

You need to understand that certain displays and seasons might require a different lighting system.

How to Wow Customers with Creative Storefront Design

Despite the significance of the storefront in retailing, too many retailers pay scant attention to this area. They spend most of their time getting the inside of their store design right and completely ignore the storefront.

For a start, the storefront window is the most expensive part of a retail space.

It is considered to be equal to one third of the entire cost of the store rental.

Robert Kretschmer reveals that, *"A small store out of the high-rent district with a rental of $100 a month, would put a yearly rental value of $400 on its window.*

Windows of the higher-class stores are often considered to be worth £20,000 a year or more.

In New York City, stores such as Macy's value their window space at more than $100,000 a year". The value of the store window is based on the number of people who pass by it each day.

When I took a trip around shopping centres in the UK, one observation I made that Kretschmer confirms in his book was that tier one retailers make proper use of their store windows. Tier two and independent retailers not knowing the value of their storefront, cover their entire storefront with discount signs.

The lower tier store directs its attention mainly to the purchaser of low-priced goods.

The windows of such a store are often crowded, more like the old-time general store.

You can further identify this type of store by its inferior price tickets and gaudy show cards and banners.

One of the most important elements of a storefront display is to tell the story of the display. Having a sign that says 70% as the only storefront display of a retail store tells customers that particular retailer has no story to tell.

The general consensus in marketing is that people buy emotionally but justify their decisions rationally. To appeal to their emotions, you should have more than your price displayed at your storefront.

Price is a single factor for which people buy and in most cases it's the least of the reasons people buy. Thirty to 40% of customers will buy on price alone. However, up to 70% will buy on the basis of convenience, good customer experience and quality.

Therefore, in order to persuade the large majority of people to enter your store, you need more than 70% discount stickers displayed at your storefront.

The storefront needs to convey a clear message about your brand and products. The message must be simple, unambiguous and to the point that shoppers get it as they walk by.

The decision to take a closer look at your display or enter your store depends on how attractive he (she) finds your storefront display.

There is a direct correlation between your storefront design and customer traffic.

Traffic will increase if your storefront is designed to catch the eyes and get in to the psyche of shoppers as they pass by your store.

The power of your storefront is as much in its signage, as it is in its lighting, interactive window displays and visual merchandise displays.

Storefronts vary from one store to the other.

Depending on the type of retailer, it can include wholesale stores, kiosks, barrows, market stalls and internet based retail stores.

However, all retail storefronts must meet the following three objectives:

- Attract shoppers attention
- Entice shoppers to enter the store
- Persuade them to buy

To meet the above objectives your storefront design must above all else, represent the image of your store.

Storefront entrance

Your door location and design are essential components of your storefront.

They are the customer's transition from the outside world to your store.

Consequently, it is advisable that doors provide direct link from the sidewalks or streets and should create a unique experience that distinguishes your store from other stores.

Storefront materials

The most appropriate materials for a storefront are:

- Wood
- Metal
- Brick
- Stone
- Glass
- Concrete

Your storefront lighting system

A well-lit storefront is a must, for the right store image.

Effective lighting is good for merchandise displays as well as the safety of your customer and the general public.

Sign lighting, including flat-mounted signs, blade and banner signs ought to be lit with covered or down lighting.

Lighting fixtures need to be positioned in such a way that they focus on the products on display not the window or street.

When lighting fixtures are not positioned well, they either distract from the display or allow shadows that interfere with the display.

Your awnings

If your store has awnings ensure it is periodically cleaned to maintain the veracity of fabrics, seam and colour.

The best types of awnings are retractable or open side as opposed to vinyl or internally lit awnings.

Signage

Your storefront signage illuminates the outside of your store and attracts customers like moths to a flame.

Here the lighting also builds a sense of branding and brand engagement.

The signage peeps into the soul of customers and creates a connection between them and your storefront signage.

Strategies for designing an attractive storefront

Display your finest merchandise in your storefront window

Display your best and newest collection of merchandise in your storefront window.

Maintain a clean storefront

Your storefront ought to be clean and tidy at all times. You need to ensure that glass windows are sparkling clean to increase visibility, bricks and mortar buildings are pressure washed, wooden buildings are treated with vanish with a gloss finish and litter, leaves or any type of dirt is constantly removed from your store entrance.

Encourage curiosity with sidewalk sales

Extending your display to outside of your store, for example in the centre of the shopping centre, stirs curiosity.

Make promotion and discount visible

This might seem to run contrary to what I said in an earlier section about displaying huge sales signs on your storefront.

Decorate storefront with plants

If possible, enhance your storefront with plants.

A retail storefront serves three main purposes:

- It is the image of the store and all that it represents
- It serves as an effective marketing tool to attract customers into the store
- It is the point of transition between the outside world and your store

Steps For Designing Attractive Storefront

Step One

Ensure your storefront is made entirely of glass with focal points, wooden cubes and shelves for merchandise.

Step Two

Fit awnings to protect shoppers viewing your displays, from rain, sun or snow.

Step Three

Install attractive and informative signage that is visible from the other side of the road and is easy to read.

Signs should be hung on the outside of the building, front door and windows.

Step Four

Decorate the pavement of the door front with attractive tiles and ensure that doorframes are big enough for all sizes of customers.

Step Five

Install adequate lighting system at your storefront.

Ensure proper lighting on display and the entrance as a whole.

Step Six

Paint your storefront with a vibrant colour; hang seasonal banners; flags or holiday decoration. Do anything that would make your storefront standout.

Remember your storefront is the best and most inexpensive marketing tool at your disposal. Make full use of it and ensure that every decision you make about your storefront design is based on sound marketing principles.

How To Choose The Right Materials For Store Design

Like most things in life, the difference between success and failure depends on doing the little things better than the rest of the field.

In retailing one of those little things is to ensure that you acquire the right materials for your store design.

The three areas of your store design you really need to focus on are:

- Ceiling
- Walls
- Floor

Ceiling

When your ceiling looks good, customers will hardly it as they enter your store.

That is a fact.

However, if it is not presentable everyone will notice it. Remember that.

Ceilings are classified in accordance with their appearance or construction.

There is:

Cathedral ceiling

Cathedral ceiling is a tall ceiling area similar to that used in churches.

Dropped ceiling

Dropped ceilings are specifically used for aesthetic or practical purposes either to achieve a certain ceiling height or to provide space for piping.

Wall Covering

The most commonly used wall covering in retail space is paint.

In addition to heavy-textured paints, the three main types of wall finishing are gloss, semi-gloss and flat.

Flat paints are suitable for walls, while gloss and semi-gloss are suitable for doors, trims and high contact areas.

Wallpaper is another type of covering used in some retail stores.

Wallpaper needs to be located in less contact areas – probably close to the ceilings.

Flooring

Flooring is another very important component of retail store design.

Unlike the ceiling, customers actually look at the flooring when they enter the store; therefore, it is imperative that you lay good flooring in your store.

Carpeting is the most widely used flooring type in the retail industry for the obvious reason that it is reasonably priced and comes in a variety of colours and textures and it has significant sound absorbing properties.

Other flooring materials used are:

- Resilient floors
- Wooded floors
- Non-resilient floors

Workshop

1. How easy is it for customers to navigate your store: walk through the ales, find what they are looking for, get assistant, reach products?

_____

_____

_____

2. Does your storefront appeal to shoppers as they walk pass it?

_____

_____

_____

3. How easy is it for customers to make payment and exist your store?

_____

_____

_____

4. Does your current design to trigger automatic upsell?

_____

_____

_____

5. What emotion does your store colour stimulate in your customer?

_____

_____

_____

6. How effective is your store lighting system, does your lighting system make to purchase process easy for your customers?

_____

_____

_____

7. Do you properly utilise the selling, service and circulation areas well?

_____

_____

_____

8. Do your customers like relaxing in your store?

_____

_____

_____

9. What design type do you have in your store, free flow, grid pattern or spin design and why did you choose that design?

_____

_____

_____

10. Are your customers able to move freely in your store?

_____

_____

_____

Module Three:

Visual Merchandising Display

How To Use Visual Merchandising to Increase Sales

Simply defined, visual merchandising display is the art and science of displaying products to influence shoppers' buying decision.

Visual Merchandising display is what shoppers see when passing by a retail store or when they are inside the store.

It creates a positive image of the store that results in attention, interest, desire and action on the part of the customer.

Good visual merchandising display in a retail store:
- Enables shoppers locate products, easily
- Keeps customers updated on the latest trends
- Influences customer buying decision
- Creates a pleasant shopping experience
- Presents the product to shoppers
- Invites the shoppers to get closer to the product
- Encourages shoppers to make a purchase
- Tells shoppers everything they need to know about products without the need to make inquiries

The following are the three display structures used in retail stores.

A retailer may choose to use the three structures, depending on the product range or depending on the targeted audience could use any of the three:

- Store-Front
- Window Display
- Found-Space Display

The most important element of visual merchandising display is the shop window display. It attracts shoppers as they walk pass and entice them to enter the store.

There are lots of people who might have no intention of shopping on a particular day.

However, the attractiveness of your window display could entice them into your store.

Window displays usually face the shopping mall or main shopping street and they are intended to attract passers-by and entice them to enter the retail store.

The storefront display is designed to build your brand image and tell the right story of your organisation.

When developing the concept for your storefront, create the design from the customer's prospective. You need to enter the customer's mind and ask yourself the question: What would my customers see when they look at my storefront display?

What would they feel as they pass by my storefront?

When planning a window display take into consideration the following:

- The building façade
- The street
- Your target market and their perceptions
- Colour harmony
- Lighting
- Viewing angles

Window displays are more successful when a central theme is carried throughout the display, whether the featured products are fashion-oriented, institutional or promotional in nature.

Window displays need to be constantly updated, preferably on a weekly basis or as often as possible. This sends a message to customers that there is always something new going on in the store.

Below are points to consider when creating store displays for increased sales:

Install signage

Store signage needs to be appropriately installed and placed in a position that allows shoppers to read the information written on them from across the aisle.

A sign is a silent salesperson and a huge part of the shopper's first impression of your store.

Use the appropriate colour

Your colour usage will significantly contribute to shoppers' impression of your store as they walk pass it. Also, the store colour needs to be suitably chosen as it can influence your customer's mood.

The wall colours need to correspond with the carpet, floor tiles or the fixtures.

Lighting system

The store should be appropriately lit and well ventilated.

Lighting increases the visibility of the merchandise.

A properly lit store contributes to the promotion of specific products and the store's image. And store window lights should be strong enough to overcome the reflections from outside.

Contextual Product Display

Group together products in their respective racks and place associated labels on the same shelves. This helps your customers to locate products easily.

The merchandise should be appropriately and neatly placed, and should not be as if falling off the shelves.

The latest trend items should be cleverly displayed on the shelves to attract customers and entice them to buy.

Expensive and unique products should be placed on the right side of the store as most people are right handed and tend to gravitate towards the right side of the store.

Old merchandise should be removed as quickly as is practicable and placed on sale to create an atmosphere of constant freshness in the store.

Identify the right furniture and fixtures

All unnecessary furniture should be removed to create enough space for customers to move freely in the store.

The more comfortable your store, the higher your chances of retaining customers, which will result in increased sales.

Use Space Sparingly

Maintaining an area for spouses or children to read or play and for physically challenged kids or elderly customers to rest also contributes to a good customer experience.

Providing resting space is a difficult concept to sell to store planners because of the cost of retail space. However, the payoff far outweighs the cost as the longer shoppers stay in your store, the higher the chances of them buying.

Have Changing Rooms

A changing room is an important component for a clothing store as it increases the possibility of the customer buying if they have had the chance of trying on the garment to ensure it fits them well.

Maintain good ambiance

The store ambience is also essential for attracting new customers and retaining existing ones.

Customers shy away from untidy stores, therefore, ensure your store is tidy at all times.

The friendlier and more relaxing you can make your store, the longer your customers will stay, and eventually make purchase.

Playing music that appeals to your target audience can have a positive effect on your customers.

Loud music is not advisable as it hinders effective communication between the customer and store associates.

Sometimes the store's appearance is a crucial factor in terms of a customer's decision to enter your store.

Ensure your store entrance is welcoming; that your visual merchandise display tells the story of your store and the merchandise display is resulting in higher sales.

Step One – Select a theme that tells the story

There need to always be a theme or story that is being communicated to your potential customers in your display.

Develop a theme around the reason why you decide to display some specific product in the window.

- Who are the characters in your display?
- Where are they going and why?
- How old are they?
- What jobs do they do?
- What merchandise would help you tell your product story better?

If the story is about living a healthy lifestyle, what could you integrate into your theme to help you silently make this point in the display?

If your story is about Christmas, Valentine or outdoor adventure, what are the details that will make your story come alive?

You can take your story to a whole new level with the use of props and mannequins.

Just as if you were writing a story, your display needs to answer these questions:

- How old are your target market?
- What work do they do?
- Where are they going?
- What season is it?

You can also provide each mannequin a name to bring it to life.

The key clearly is to understand for whom you are creating the display and what message you want to convey through the display.

Step Two – Know thy customer

One of the major reasons for the failure of most retail ventures is that most retailers do not know their target market.

This is marketing 101: It is critical for your success as a business.

If you do not know who you serve, you might not be serving anyone.

- Who are your costumers?
- Are they teenagers, young professionals, college students or young couples?
- Are they homemakers?
- Are they Single mums?
- Are they women in their 40's with lots of discretionary income?
- Do your customers want a bargain or are they looking for something unique?
- What interests them?

Step Three – Identify your Competitors

It is critical that you know your competitors, their product offering and service provision.

By having an understanding of the strength and weaknesses of your competition, you can better prepare a display that either directly rivals or is better than theirs.

Step Four – Choose the right products for your store window

Your storefront is a window to your store.

Products displayed provide potential customers an idea of the products inside the store.

Consequently, it is imperative that you choose the products that are displayed in the shop window carefully.

You need to display products that are the most representative of products in your store.

Step Five – Observe the effect of display on your customers

An effective way to attract customers is to have good exterior and interior displays.

As customers pass by your display, you need to have a procedure for measuring the effect of your display on them.

- Does your display window inspire your customers?
- Is it pleasing to the eye and does it have a welcoming effect?

Ensure you display your merchandise as it would be used in a real life scenario and that it is kept simple but striking to ensure maximum impact.

The key to increasing retail sales; is an impressive and eye catching presentation of merchandise that attracts shoppers as they pass by your store.

Challenges Visual Merchandisers Face

Changing customer buying behaviour

The changing dynamic of the target audience is one of the greatest challenges facing visual merchandisers.

The volatility of consumer behaviour creates a nightmarish scenario for visual merchandisers who constantly have to invent creative ways to attract potential customers' attention.

Constant new products

The constant development of new products, scarcity of display space allocation and the constant change in consumer preferences, all add to the challenging environment for visual merchandisers.

Solution

One way of dealing with this challenge is to:

Reserve a specific section of the store for testing products.

The only products that will be displayed in this section would be new products.

This would make it easy for visual merchandisers and customers.

Limited Display Space

Retail space is expensive; therefore, every inch of the store's display space has to be used to its maximum.

However, with the constant introduction of new products, even hyper-stores struggle for space to accommodate all of the new products.

Solution

The best solution would be to place as much variety as possible but in small quantities.

Store staff need to keep constant watch on shelves to ensure they are not empty and are faced up.

Supplier demand Premium Spacing

Suppliers compete to have their products displayed in the most prominent and high traffic locations in the store. Here you must be alert for signs of conflict of interest between senior management, visual merchandisers and other store staff.

Solution

Suppliers and senior retail management need to be educated on the function of visual merchandising display in a retail store.

How to Burst the Price Myth with Creative Merchandise Display

I am a one-click buyer in Amazon. I buy a lot of books because of my line of work.

I was pleasantly surprised to learn that I could even buy white board and all my stationary from Amazon.

I cannot remember the last time I entered a bookstore.

I have a lot of friends like me who do the majority of their shopping online.

They shop for clothes and even groceries online.

Why do I and many of the people do our shopping online?

We are sold on the convenience.

The 18th century was about speed of production in order to increase capacity.

The 19th century focused on quality.

With increased production leading to over capacity, the focus shifted from speed to quality.

In the 21st century, the focus has shifted from quality to value and total customer experience. But many retailers have failed to grasp this concept.

Here is the secret, despite the fact that people conduct research online, the large majority still don't trust information found online.

That is why books are still highly rated even though the information in most books can be found online.

People still trust other people and prefer to interact with people.

So despite the internet, bricks and mortar retailing will survive.

However, there is a new dynamic and retailers need to understand this.

The consumer of today is better informed than the consumer of ten or twenty years ago. Consequently, today's retail staff need to be better informed than retail staff of ten or twenty years ago.

One cannot navigate the 21st century with a 19th century skill set – it will not work.

Even in recession hit Greece and Spain, the luxury retail market continues to flourish.

The explanation that most people would have for this is that the rich keep getting richer.

Even though this might be true, this is not the main reason for the continued buoyancy of the luxury retail market.

The explanation lies in the fact that luxury retailers take the concept of total customer experience to the extreme.

When you visit Harrods, there is a store assistant within an arm's length of each and every customer.

On the other hand when you visit some retail stores, you can hardly find anyone to speak to when you need help.

I told the story of being forced to leave Next because I could not find a store assistant to offer me assistance.

I have news for Next, there are lots of people like myself who might have left Next for the same reason.

I hope you are taking note too.

To succeed in the 21st century retail environment, it is the little things that make the difference.

As a retailer, if you still believe that price is what is going to entice people to your store and make you successful, you are on the wrong end of the stick.

21st century retail is about value and total customer experience. An essential component of a value driven strategy is an attractive visual merchandising display.

As Michael Porter puts it, *"cutting prices is usually insane if the competition can go as low as you can"*.

If price reduction is your main strategy for increasing your sales, then you have already lost.

Maintaining pricing integrity can be challenging in the face of fierce competition.

But it can turn out to be a smart business decision in the long run.

The concept of value is perceptive.

What constitutes value to one person might not be that valuable to another.

However, there is a universal perception about value that exists in the mind of every customer: cheap is poor quality and expensive is high quality.

Despite the fact that this concept has proven time and time again to be untrue, like most things in life, it is the perception that matters.

Step One

Identify and understand your target market. Like in the case of Harrods, customers visit a particular store for a reason. Your job is to find out who your customers are and what they want.

Step Two

Instead of discounting your current line, you could consider resizing.

An alternative to discounting is offering lower price for a smaller size.

Probably there are ways that you could repackage your products that make financial sense to discount, without eating into your profit margin.

Step Three

Emphasize benefits of the products instead of the price.

There is no getting away from the fact that it is very difficult to differentiate one commodity from the other. But it can be done if the retailer places emphasis on other intangible aspects of the buying decision.

Step Four

Emphasize the soft aspect of your offering such as:

- Great customer service
- Knowledgeable staff
- Easy access to merchandise
- Easy to locate merchandise
- An easy to navigate store

This might sound trivial, but in marketing, it is the things that are over-looked that count. The everyday thing that you think might not be important to customers may well be what is important to them.

The price discounting game is a losing one, do not play it, it is not a good business strategy.

The best antidote in a price driven market such as retail is to focus on a value driven strategy, instead of a price driven strategy.

As I pointed out in the case of Harrods and the luxury retail market that is flourishing, despite the economic downturn, price is never a good differentiator; therefore, it is imprudent for it to be used as a long-term business strategy.

In this 21st century customer centrist environment, the definition of value has shifted from seller to the customer.

Competition is fierce and the monopolisation of the factors of distribution has been broken leaving the field wide open for anyone to enter. Now, success as a retailer would is no longer dependent on 19th century marketing strategies.

Succeeding in retail in the 21st century requires rethinking your approach to services provision. *It is now about providing sustainable, durable, reliable and high quality products at reasonable price.*

The Best Merchandise Display Strategy

Visual merchandising display is basically the physical presentation of products for the purpose of increasing sales.

Visual merchandising is essential for maintaining the balance between shelf and warehouse stock.

Visual merchandising display is commonly referred to as the silent salesman because a good display effectively sells the products.

The core objectives of visual merchandising are to:

- Enable shoppers to examine products closely
- Maintain the customer's interest in the product
- Encourage them to lower their psychological defences
- Make the purchasing decision easy

However, the most successful retailers do not view visual merchandising as just the display of products on the shop floor. They see it as a marketing tool.

The main objective of a visual merchandise display is to motivate customer interest in your products.

Displays should also be able to provide information about the products; show customers how to use the product.

A good visual merchandise display strategy answers the following questions:

- Does the display fit your brand image?
- Is it attractive enough to capture the customer's attention?
- Does it have a story to tell to the customer?
- Does it have a clear and specific message for the customer?
- Is it focused on the product?
- Is the information on the display easy to read?
- Does the lighting system bring out the best in the display?
- Is the display well organised?

A creative visual merchandise display must have the following:

Balance

Balance refers to the manner in which the products are arranged around an imaginary centreline.

When the phrase formal balance is discussed in relation to a visual merchandise display, it means that a product is on one side of the line, and a similar product is displayed at the same distance from the line between both products in the display.

Balance encompasses the symmetry and weight of products on two sides of a display.

Emphasis

Emphasis is using one product in the display as the centre of attraction.

The product would be core of the display around which the rest of the display is arranged.

Proportion

Proportion is the dimension and spacing of products in a display.

Proportion can refer to the relationship between the product used as emphasis and the rest of the products in the display.

Rhythm

Rhythm is the measurement of systematised movement from one product to the next, in a merchandise display.

Rhythm is an inexplicit guide tactically placed in the display to guide the customer's eyes from product to product, back to front and/or side to side.

Harmony

Harmony conveys the mood and emotions of the display. It is obviously the most important aspect of the display.

However, because it is not a tangible object, its essence could be lost in the display.

Harmony is the story and message within the products on display. It is what brings the display to life and gives it character.

Display Needs Concept

What's the concept?

What is the concept of the display? What would it be communicating to your target market?

The most effective displays are the ones in which the products are displayed exactly how they are to be used.

It could be a clothing display in which the item is dressed on a mannequin the way someone it is expected to wear them.

The display structure

Consideration has to be given to the area in which the display is to be located.

The location of the display has a significant impact on how it is to be arranged?

In retail, store displays are usually located in windows, on walls, cases, gondolas or islands.

The specific area in which the display is to be located within the store would determine its size and shape.

Promotional displays

Displays created for promotional purposes need to be different from the rest of the displays in the store. They need to be located in the front of the store for a short period after which if you intend on carrying on the display for a long time, they should be moved to the back of the store.

Step One – Determine the goal of the display

Every display needs to have a specific goal.

The questions with which to determine this are:

- Is the goal of the display to promote new products?
- To carry on promotion
- To attract a new target market to your store?

There needs to be a goal for each and every display.

Step Two – Choose the right merchandise

The merchandise on display needs to reflect the types of merchandise you sell.

To ensure this takes place, here are the questions you need to answer:

- Does the merchandise on display match the quality of your product?
- Does it reflect your brand image?

Your merchandise displays need to contain the right product for the right time.

If the display is for Valentine, every product on the display needs to be related to valentine.

Step Three – Choose a theme

Every display needs to have a theme.

The theme of the display is the story behind the display.

You need to be able to identify the message you want the display to send to your target market.

The theme of your merchandising can be a way to communicate a seasonal message to your target market.

Step Four – Select Props

Props are the items used in a merchandise display to physically support the merchandise that form part of the display theme.

Props are essential for strengthening the message of a display.

Prop characters are essential for determining the overall appearance and feel of a display hence the reason why it is essential to get the appropriate props for your display.

Step Five – Create a contextual display

Create contextual displays by merging similar products together.

This makes buying decisions easier for customers. For example: putting together shirt and ties or shoes and socks.

When products are grouped, they make it easier for customers to choose.

It also results in increased sales as it encourages impulse buying.

Step Six – Develop Signs

Ensure your signage is visible enough to complement the merchandise on display.

There needs to a balance in the amount of signage placed on a display, to avoid confusion.

The objective of signage in a display is to provide information such as the price of the products on display. It needs to be brief and easy to read.

Step Seven – Design the lighting

Your lighting system is the most important element of your display.

You need to ensure that the lighting system used for your display is the most appropriate one.

The lighting system is also very crucial for your display, because the right lighting system enhances the appearance of the products.

A good lighting system can also create an illusion and make products in the display appear more valuable than they actually are.

Finally, displays must be neat and simple. A cluttered display sends a bad impression of your store while a confusing display would result in poor sales.

Therefore, it is very important that displays are:

- Neat
- Uncluttered, and
- The display area clean
- There are no unrelated things lying about

How to Maximise Display Space Allocation with Creative Display

Maximising display space to achieve the maximum return on investment per square foot ought to be a main objective of your visual merchandising display strategy.

The cost of retail space by square foot is on the increase. So too is the variation of products.

Creative use of display space is particularly relevant for retailers who sell low value products.

There are only so many products that can be crammed on a shelf in a small retail space. This means that to ensure maximum profit for the retailer, space needs to be used creatively.

The efficient use of retail display space has several benefits:

- The ability to stock more products

    The more space you have to display merchandise the more products you can display in your store.

- More supplier support

    With fierce competition in the retail marketplace, all suppliers want their products to be allocated a space in a store, preferably in the high traffic areas. Consequently, suppliers are willing to bargain for marketing support and higher space rental, just to get the space that they want.

- More organised and controlled displays

An organised and well-controlled display area results in the maximisation of space. When your store is well organised it is easier to monitor your products. There are also fewer incidents of pilferage and theft.

- Increased consumer satisfaction

  Aside from good quality products and services that the store offers, availability is also very important to the consumer. Product prices prove irrelevant in comparison to convenience and quality.

- Increased sales and profit

  Increased customer satisfaction results in increased sales and profit. Word of mouth advertisement based on personal experience is the oldest but still the most effective marketing tool.

- It helps prevent out-of stock and inadvertently, loss of sales

  When you display your merchandise properly on the shop floor, it can be easily monitored by staff to ensure that the spaces are constantly refilled.

The effectiveness of a visual merchandise display space would depend on a few key factors:

- The type of merchandise you sell
- The location of the building
- Your store design
- The amount you are willing to allocate to the process

One-third of the products in an average retail store each year are new.

Each new product brings with it the accompanying challenge of finding a suitable spot on the shop floor.

To ensure an effective use of your display space, consider the following:

Set a realistic budget

Your budget is the first thing you need to consider. How much will you realistically spend on visual merchandising; knowing fully well the benefits of the process?

Create a blueprint

A blueprint of your display space taking into account your product line is another point for thought when developing your visual merchandising display plan.

Plan the traffic flow

Customers need to be able to properly examine the products from all angles to make an informed buying decision.

Ensure you allow sufficient space for aisles and give consideration to the projected traffic flow.

Remember, you would want your customers to move through your display areas and to the checkout counter with ease.

How to use space well

In retail, space means money. The store has to be designed in such a way that it optimises the selling area and minimises non-selling areas.

The selling area is used to present the merchandise and the non-selling section is taken up by passage space, aisles, staircases, lifts, facilities, and the back area.

The average area mix in a department store is: selling area about 65%, circulation area 15% and back area 20%.

Step One – Get the appropriate space and product assortment

Retailers optimise and rationalise their assortments based on enhanced analysis of profitability and the apprehension that variety may be over-whelming for customers.

Step Two – Systematize strategies to manage space

You should re-evaluate your business operations; standardise new and revise older formats.

You should competently segment and align your retail space to consumer needs and purchasing behaviour.

Step Three – Integrate online and offline channels

The increasing importance of online shopping is changing notions of space management.

It introduces the concept of the "endless aisle" and encourages retailers to treat the internet as an integral part of their operations.

Plan your display strategies

When planning your display space, you need to take into account the following:

- The average person's field of vision tends to be around 170 degrees
- The number of product categories in the store
- The percentage of space to be allotted to each category
- The volume of merchandise in each category
- The relative placement of each category

Here are a few things to consider when allocating display space:

Fixture arrangement

One of the most common fixtures in stores is the gondola – movable shelving that are accessible from all sides.

They should be lined up in rows as in grocery, hardware and drug stores or used singly to form an island.

When placing racks, progress from small fixtures to large fixtures near the back walls.

When working with hard goods, place cubes in the front with gondolas to the rear of the department or store.

Higher end stores require fewer fixtures because there are less merchandise.

Use primarily T-stands and four ways to create an illusion of space for selective goods.

Contextual Merchandising

Similar merchandise should be grouped together on the end-cap and gondola sides.

The end-cap should indicate the type of related merchandise on the gondola sides.

For example, golf balls displayed on an end-cap should indicate that related golf accessories are located on gondola sides.

Centralise high-ticket products

Customers usually look to the centre of gondola sides first before looking either to the left or right.

Additional high-ticket impulse items should be placed in the centre of gondola sides and other related merchandise to either the left or right.

Larger more expensive merchandise should be placed to the right.

Furthermore, high-ticket items should be placed at eye level.

Allow contact

If possible, remove a sample from packaging to allow customers to touch and feel the item.

Old merchandise should be cleaned and pulled forward as new merchandise is added to the display.

Create rainbow presentation

Make stimulating displays with mass merchandise by using quantity and colour.

A good way of arranging merchandise on a gondola is by colour.

People think of colours in a rainbow pattern and are comfortable with that sort of presentation.

Display merchandise in quantity on quads, round and T-stands; use cubes for folded goods.

Use geometric pattern

A well-planned geometric aisle pattern works best to maximize sales.

Place aisle displays in an island rather than wing fixtures.

Fixtures that work well for sale items include tub tables, round racks and rectangular racks lay product. Allow need to be three feet between racks.

Leave fire exit free

The aisle leading directly to the fire exit is considered a major aisle.

Do not block the fire exit with fixtures or extraneous materials.

Legal requirements for aisle width vary from four to eight feet.

The most common aisle width is six feet.

Check your local codes for your local requirements.

Your goal should be to have enough products on display, not overcrowded fixtures and walls. In addition, clearly delineate product categories.

Maximising fixture practice requires fresh eyes and a creative spirit alongside a desire to drive sales.

The Benefits Planogram Software

A planogram is a marketing instrument used in retail stores.

It is an illustration or drawing that provides details of where a product should be placed on a shelf and how many facing that product should have.

It is used by a retail store to increase sales and by suppliers to justify the space allocated of brands and new products.

Retailers employ planograms to enable the come up with product displays that draw customers' interest and help them increase their sales.

The complexity of a planogram may differ by the size of store, the software used to create the planogram and the needs of the retailer.

Why is planogram good for visual merchandising?

Planograms are an accurate way of presenting new ideas for product placement, testing merchandising principles and understanding best possible inventory requirements.

It is a schematic of shelving and fixtures and positioning of products on those shelves or fixtures.

Successful retail space planning and management is an important part of the merchandise planning and execution.

A well-designed shopping environment catches the attention of customers; prevents stock outs, enhances inventory productivity, reduces operating costs and most of all boosts the financial performance of the store.

Here are the advantages of utilising a planogram for visual merchandising:

Guaranteed product placement
Accurate store-specific planograms ensure optimum supply-chain efficiency that results in higher availability to shoppers, maximum stock turn over and ensures efficient use of space.

Improved sales
Targeted store-specific planograms direct maximum in-store compliance, resulting in an accurate understanding of product distribution that eventually increase sales.

Tighter inventory control and reduction of stock outs
Focused store-specific planograms lead to increased sales and profitability, easier product replenishment, reduction in stock and operational costs and an overall enhancement in bottom line contribution.

Satisfying customers with a better visual appeal
Improves customer satisfaction by making it easier to shop in shelves that are well organised and reduces the time it takes to arrange stock in the store.

Influence customer behaviour for trade-up and impulse buying, which result in increased sales.

Effective communication tool for staff

Tailors assortments including product launches and group specific go-to-market strategies so that you can improve cluster, meet true local demand and effectively communicate with your staff.

Assigned selling potential to every inch of retail space

Enables better management of inventory by allocating shelf space and facings based on movement, which in turn reduces out-of-stocks; streamlines space and floor planning, so that you can increase your space productivity and optimise your capital investment.

Merchandising Tactics

Improved merchandising best practices by testing and comparison of cause and effect in like stores; translates merchandising strategy into tactics; so that you can drive consistent store execution of your corporate strategic and assortment decisions.

Planograms will give you a good idea of how a display will look before you physically dress that merchandise on the shelves in your store.

Planograms can be as easy as a photo of a pre-set section or more thorough with numbered peg holes and shelf notches showing the exact position of each item.

Below are some things to consider when implementing planogram in your store:

Quality

Includes shelf heights, merchandise placement and the quantity of facings.

Shelf heights depend on the volume of the products and ease of reach for customers.

Importance

The arrangement and number of facings merchandise has will considerably change its sales at the store.

It will also change the store's overall performance.

Purpose

The objective of the planogram is to increase sales and offer the most popular product the best spot to attract customers.

A store should regularly modify the layout of all of its fixtures.

Time Schedule

Planograms are typically planned a few weeks in advance of their implementation.

Listed below are the types of commonly used planograms:

Box with text

The most basic form of planograms utilise box shapes to represent different goods, with the name of the item typed inside the box.

Pictorial

Pictorial planogram is normally used in clothing and department stores wherein displays are more important and arrangement is essential.

3-D

Planogram application differs by retail sector.

Three-dimensional planograms are usually drawn to scale and include aerial views of the area.

Planned Category

Customers might need a product but prior to going to the store have not determined which brand, size, quantity and flavour they require.

Having planned category helps to make the customer's decision easier.

Impulse buying

A customer might not have plans to buy an item, but seeing the item on display might trigger their desire to buy it.

Substitution

An appropriately merchandised planogram can influence trade-up or trade-down purchases.

For example, a customer originally plans to purchase Brand 'A' but proper planogramming directs the customer to Brand 'B' which is offered as a better value choice.

Triggered

Busy customers frequently appear at the store knowing what they want to purchase; they just don't have a specific list.

A "triggered" purchase takes place when they see the product on the shelf which serves as a reminder, which encourage them to buy.

Contextual

Making sure that product category is accurately placed with the aid of correct planogramming will lead to larger transactions and happier consumers.

What can you do in your store right now to implement a planogram?

Here are some things to consider.

Location

Where in the store located?

Are there secondary placements?

Category Space Allocation

How much space will be allocated to each category?

Product Space

What will space allocation be based on: Sales, movement, mandates or inventory thresholds?

Layout

What will the planogram structured be based on: Price, brand or manufacturers?

Labels/ Signage

How would the category or section benefit from signage or point of purchase materials?

Planogram makes the work of your employees easy at store level. As they do not need to think about where products are to be placed, it increases staff productivity and decreases shrinkage.

Workshop

1. What is the concept of the display? Does it have theme and character?

_____

_____

_____

2. What message does your display communicate to your target market? Who are they? Where are they going and why? How old are they? What jobs do they do?

_____

_____

_____

3. What is the story of your display? What merchandise would help you tell your product story better? If the story is about living a healthy lifestyle, what could you integrate into your theme to help you silently make this point in the display? If your story is about Christmas, Valentine or outdoor adventure, what (details) will make your story come alive?

_____

_____

4. Just as if you were writing a story, your display needs to answer these questions: What's the average age of you target market? What do they do? Where are they going? What season is it? Does your display answer those questions?

_____

_____

_____

5. When planning a window display do you take into consideration the following: the building façade, the street, your target market and their perceptions, colour harmony, lighting or viewing angles?

_____

_____

_____

6. Do you group products together in their respective racks and place associated labels on the same shelves?

_____

_____

_____

7. It is critical that you know your competitors, their product offering and service provision. By having an understanding of the strength and weaknesses of your competition, you can better prepare a display that either directly rivals or is better than theirs. Do you know your competitors?

_____

_____

_____

8. As you are aware, retail space is expensive; therefore, every inch of the store's display space has to be used to its maximum. How efficiently do you use your display space?

_____

_____

_____

9. Do you emphasize the soft aspect of your offering such as great customer service, knowledgeable staff, easy access to merchandise, easy to locate merchandise or an easy to navigate store as part of your marketing?

_____

_____

_____

10. Do you use planogram software for your display? Why do you use planogram? Which type of planogram do you use? What benefits do your derive from using planogram software?

_____

_____

_____

Module Four:

How to Increase Retail Profit with Effective Loss Prevention Strategies

Why do you need to reduce your shrinkage?

You need to reduce your shrinkage because the average retailer makes a 1% net profit out of each pound and in retail, the industry shrinkage level is 2.6%.

What this means is your shrinkage percentage is almost three times your profit margin.

Therefore, if you reduced your shrinkage by 50% – from 2.6 cents to 1.3 cents, you could more than double your profits: from 1 cent to 2.3 cents.

Let me briefly repeat this point because it is so important.

Right now, your profit margin is 1%.

Your average shrinkage level is 2.6%, so reducing your shrinkage level by 50% to 1.3% can increase your profit margin to 2.6%.

Retail is a strange business; it is the only business where profit is not a priority.

Even charities and religious organisations know if they don't make a profit, they will go out of business.

When other businesses produce their annual or quarterly reports, the reports are based on profit and loss.

However, at the end of each quarter when many retail organisations give their performance report, the emphasis is on like-for-like sales.

Profit is mentioned as something of a side issue; or by the way, we made this percentage profit.

It is no surprise therefore that the moment there is a slight jolt in the economy many retailers go out of business.

If a business has 1% profit margin and it does not do everything within it powers to reduce losses, it is only a matter of time before it goes out of business.

Many UK High Streets are still a ghost town, despite efforts by the government to prop up the industry.

The problem with government's attempt, like most government funded initiatives, the focus is on the symptom rather than the root cause of the problem. Limited or lack of profit is the simple explanation many retailers are struggling or going bust. Even Tesco, once the second most profitable retailer in the world and the fourth most profitable business in the UK is struggling to match year on year profit.

For the second year in a row Tesco's profit has dropped, sending shareholders and the markets into a frenzy.

I believe what they really need to be worrying about is the statement by the CEO in which he hinted; he was going to abandon the company's profit target of 5.2%.

This is a direct quote from him: *"follow the customer and the margins will be what they will be"*

If he was a football manager, he will probably be under a bus by now.

This is a complete U-turn from his predecessor whose focus was entirely on profit, which was the reason Tesco achieved that level of success under his stewardship. Tesco's current CEO's attitude to profit is the attitude of typical retail chief executives. They focus exclusively on sales, at the expense of profit.

I know I named this workbook 'how to increase retail sales'. But my idea of increasing sales is not at the expense of profit.

My goal is to ensure you increase your store sales and profit simultaneously.

So why do you do need to increase your profit? You need to increase your profit margin because business is about profit.

If profit is not the KPI of any business, the owner wants to consider doing something different.

It is only when you make profit you will have the resources to reinvest and grow your business, such as investing in your marketing and other activities that will result in profit.

The easiest way to make profit in retail is to reduce your shrinkage level.

There are two reasons why shrinkage reduction is the simplest way of increasing retail profit.

Firstly, you cannot control sales. There are lots of things you can do to influence the outcome of your marketing efforts. However, you are still at the mercy of market forces.

But when it comes to shrinkage reduction, you have complete control over the outcome.

This brings us to the second point. In the large majority of cases, shrinkage is caused by the absence of the right policies and procedures.

Simply making a few changes to your current policies and procedures can reduce your shrinkage level by as much as 84%.

Lessons from My Tesco Experience

To hammer home this point further; let me tell you my experience of my work with Tesco.

I worked as a stock controller for fresh food. We were hired to help with expansion of the store. At first, they gave us the usual few hours training in the training room.

So when I was assigned to fresh food, I had to be retrained to be able to work in the fresh food department. My trainer was a guy I will call Dani, which is not his real name. He quickly brought me up to speed on how to take stock in the fresh food department. He taught me some pretty good and not so good stuff.

For example, most of the time, we never bothered to go to the back of the freezer to check the stock.

Normally the ideal way of selling fresh food is on a first come first serve basis. Old stock needs to be sold before fresh stock.

However, because we were unwilling to go to the back of the freezer to get fresh stock, we displayed stock as they arrived so the old ones remained in the freezer and when they expired, they were thrown away. It did not help that we had no supervision. The Stock Control Manager was perpetually absent.

When he showed up for work, which he seldom did, he had absolutely no interest in what was going in the department.

So why did I tell this story?

Certainly not to disparage Tesco but to emphasise the point that shrinkage is manmade.

If Tesco has a structural training process for new employees like me, the shrinkage that was caused because Dani taught me the wrong stuff would not have taken place.

And if the Stock Control or Store Managers paid attention to what was happening in the department, they would have discovered the things we were doing.

Multiply the number of Danis by the number of Tesco stores, and you see how much Tesco was and may still be losing.

When I read reports about retailers that go bust or into administration, not a single one of them mentions the fact that they had high shrinkage levels. The excuse is always lack of sales or difficult trading conditions.

It never occurs to them that if they were making profit in the first instance they would not be affected by difficult trading conditions.

What I aim to do in this workbook is to point out the ways retail stores are losing unnecessary money through shrinkage and suggest ways of stemming them.

Why are Retail Organisations Still Failing to Reduce Shrinkage?

There are two reasons why retail organisations have not been able to have a handle on their shrinkage. The first reason as I said at the start, the retail industry does not focus on making profit. The focus is always on making sales.

If they focused on profit, they would realise that to increase sales without stemming profit-draining activities is false economy.

Secondly, most of the loss prevention methods currently in place in many retail organisations are wrong.

The reason for this is, the majority of retail loss prevention bosses are ex-services personnel, who bring the law enforcement approach to a problem that has little to do with criminality.

The large majority of retail shrinkage is the result of procedural errors within the retail organisation.

Shrinkage in the retail lexicon is another word for *shoplifting or employee theft*.

When they think about shrinkage, the only thing many retailers think about is shoplifting and employee theft.

Yes, it is true that shoplifting and employee theft account for a large percentage of retail shrinkage.

However, shoplifting and employee theft are a symptom of deeper procedural problems within the organisation.

When you deal with the procedural error, you will stem shoplifting or employee theft.

Shoplifting and retail employee theft, are crimes of opportunity; you remove the opportunity and you remove the possibility.

This workbook will focus on:

- How to create a culture of loss prevention
- How to prevent employee theft
- How to prevent employee error
- How to create an efficient receiving process
- How to prevent perishable shrinkage
- How to prevent non-perishable shrinkage
- How to prevent shoplifting

How to Create a Culture of Loss Prevention

What is retail shrinkage?

Shrinkage is the loss in value of the goods from the time they are received by the store, to the point of sale. I am sure not a lot of retailers define shrinkage in such a manner. For them shrinkage is shoplifting and employee theft.

Yes, shoplifting and employee theft are responsible for a large part of shrinkage, but shrinkage is a combination of factors that largely result from inadequate or non-existent policies and procedures.

Shrinkage includes:

- Administrative errors
- Receiving error, fraud and theft
- Vendor error, fraud and theft
- Employee theft and error
- Procedural errors (And of course)
- Shoplifting

However, when the average retailer decides to address shrinkage, its focus is on shoplifting and employee theft.

Even when it's tries to address these issues, it deals with the symptom instead of the root cause.

To prevent shoplifting, they contract security officers. Indeed security officer at the entrance of a retail store can serve as a deterrent to amateur shoplifters. Security officers do not prevent harden shoplifters from carrying on their activities.

These days, a large percentage of shoplifting is conducted by organised retail crime syndicates. These are professional gangs who are not deterred by weak looking security officer, stood at your entrance. They are well organised and they plan well. It is like a profession for them, so they do it well. Therefore, in order to take on such a group, it has to be done from the root.

Changing policies and procedures that allow their activities to take place is the first place to start with.

I have given you a list of activities that result in shrinkage.

It is not an exhaustive list.

You noticed from the list that shoplifting and employee theft are just two of the six activities that result in shrinkage.

Being aware of the fact that your shrinkage is the result of your policies and procedures, reducing your store shrinkage requires you to first change your current policies and procedures.

It requires the creation of a culture of loss prevention in your retail store. A culture in which every single person from the CEO to the cleaner is responsible for shrinkage reduction and profit protection.

To hire a security contractor to go into your organisation to use security measures to prevent something that needs to be handled by procedural changes is a waste of resources.

Retail shrinkage is not a security issue and cannot be effectively dealt with using security measures.

It is an administrative issue that can only be dealt with by creating a culture of loss prevention.

How do you create a culture of loss prevention?

To create a culture of loss prevention, you need to take the following steps:

1. Gain senior management commitment

Senior management must first and foremost realise the concept of loss prevention is basically profit protection.

Therefore, loss prevention should never be an isolated department, it ought to be an integral part of your operations.

The annual goal for increasing sales and profit must align with the goal to decrease shrinkage.

Senior management need to communicate the importance of shrinkage reduction to their regional managers who will in turn translate this to store managers, supervisors and store associates.

Senior management need to communicate the fact that low shrinkage, equals high profit and high profit means job security for everyone.

You need to change the name of your loss prevention department to profit protection department.

Why?

Because profit protection is a series of activities geared towards inventory and asset protection, which ultimately result in sustainable profit.

So if you have a loss prevention department, I will suggest the first thing you do is to change the name of the department from loss prevention to profit protection.

There is nothing like preventing loss but protecting your profit.

That's the first step for creating a culture of loss prevention.

The use of the right terminology can completely change people's perception.

2. Train employees

Despite the fact that there are cost implications associated with training employees, an educated workforce will pay dividends in the long run compared to an uneducated one.

Everyone who has been to university knows that the one thing you are taught in university is how to think.

This is because when you know how to think you can execute better.

Training retail staff to think and execute better, can make a tremendous difference to the success of any retail organisation.

For example, the table below demonstrates that providing employees with shoplifting awareness training is a more effective tool against shoplifting than any other measure employed.

Method	Effectiveness
Employees	33%
Cameras	31%
Management	17%
EAS	14%
Signs	3%
Guards	2%

As the table shows, employees trained in shoplifting prevention were more effective at shoplifting prevention than any other method used.

They were more effective than CCTV cameras and way more effective than security officers.

3. Measure the scale of the problem

How many store managers or senior retail managers know the scale of their shrinkage problem?

How many really know which department of their store is responsible for the highest amount of shrinkage?

Step one for shrinkage reduction requires an accurate assessment of the causes, effects and costs of shrinkage.

At the beginning of a financial year, retail financial planners estimate a figure they consider an acceptable level of loss.

As long as store managers stay within this figure, it is acceptable by senior management.

This approach does not encourage store managers to investigate the causes of shrinkage or take personal responsibility for shrinkage within the bounds of the budgeted figure, set by senior management. In their minds senior management have already given their approval to those numbers.

Shrinkage prevention and reduction requires a systematic approach, which begins with:

A thorough internal inventory of all merchandise within the store, both in the warehouse and shop floor.

The implementation of policies and procedures for receiving merchandise, theft and fraud control and error prevention.

A comprehensive analysis of these areas will present a clearer picture of the stores' current problem, allowing store managers the opportunity to implement the most appropriate mechanisms for dealing with their shrinkage challenges.

4. Accurate management of accounts

Detailed and accurate transactional reports are vital as they show top management and store managers the monetary values of shrinkage.

Management accounts detailing profit and loss enable management to assess their performance and pin point areas for improvement.

5. Create awareness

The organisation's policies and procedures regarding loss prevention and shrinkage management must be constantly communicated to every single employee within the organisation.

Top management have the ability to shape the behaviour and actions of their employees by effective communication, which clearly outlines managements' goal for shrinkage reduction.

This is the 'carrot and stick' approach in which employees are made aware of the benefits that will accrue to them for cooperating while at the same time making it absolutely clear that management adopts a zero tolerance stance on shrinkage.

6. Continuous education and discipline

Any improvement in any area of life, is not an event, it requires daily practice. The same theory applies to shrinkage reduction.

In order for it to be effective, it needs to be reinforced by top management on a daily basis.

Store managers and team members need to acquire the requisite training whilst managers need to lead by example by ensuring their daily actions do not contradict their policies.

Top management need to show their commitment by providing the resources that store management require, whilst allowing operational staff the opportunity to assist in the creation of the appropriate policies and procedures.

7. Create mechanism for monitoring compliance

People do not voluntarily submit to authority or comply with rules and regulations.

It is important that senior management understand that it is human nature to do what is fun and easy.

Unfortunately, most of the activities that produce results are not fun and easy to accomplish. People therefore may shy away from those activities and focus on tasks that are easy to complete.

Senior management must keep a constant vigil on the activities of their employees. The best way of accomplishing this is to communicate regularly with store management and supervisors to identify employees that are in need of additional support.

Regular employee appraisals and daily evaluations will identify those employees who would benefit from additional support and training.

This operational practice is one of the most important as it ensures preventative measures are implemented before an issue becomes a problem.

8. Set measurable targets

Goals that get measured get achieved.

The human mind is a goal-seeking organism that operates best when it has a target to aim towards.

Senior management need to establish a form of measurement through which staff can measure their progress.

When staff can focus on daily, weekly, monthly and annual targets for shrinkage reduction, they will have a goal to aim towards.

The statistics need to be published in the staff room on a regular basis for all employees to see, as this will provide motivation for them.

When staff are motivated and aiming towards a common goal they are willing to give of their best.

Targets set must be SMARTER:

S	Specific
M	Measurable
A	Achievable
R	Realistic
T	Time-Based
E	Evaluated
R	Reviewed

9. Take advantage of technology

It can be difficult to quantify the benefit of technology.

Many technology providers struggle to explain the return on investment (ROI) for their products.

It is the exact opposite when it comes to loss prevention technologies.

The latest loss prevention technologies have transformed the retail industry.

From the time the technology device is installed to the point where retailers begin to accrue benefit, is shorter than in any other industry.

Loss prevention technologies provide an amazing 50% ROI within a very short space of time.

The retail industry is a fiercely competitive sector that is changing rapidly.

Practices and procedures can change dramatically with the introduction of a single technological device.

Technology has made the receiving and auditing processes more accurate, and ordering and forecasting easier.

However, technology must be tailored to support the issues of each individual store.

Technology on its own is not a cure.

We need to ensure that relevant training and support is offered to all levels of employees who are expected to use the devices.

10. Make adjustments to current policies and procedures

One of my favourite children's' show is Winnie the Pooh. And my favourite quotation from it goes like this:

"Here is Edward Bear, coming downstairs now, bump, bump, and bump, on the back of his head, behind Christopher Robin. It is, as far as he knows, the only way of coming downstairs, but sometimes he feels there really is another way, if only he could stop bumping for a moment and think of it". (A. A. Milne, Winnie the Pooh).

There is a better way to increase retail sales.

You can increase your store sales without sacrificing your profit.

You need to consider changing your policies and procedure to try the new information.

The old policies and procedures have not worked for many retail organisations; it's time for a change.

Workshop

As the owner or senior management, are you engaged with your loss prevention department?

_____

_____

_____

Are your loss prevention activities mainly focused on apprehending shoplifters or dishonest employees?

_____

_____

_____

Do you know the actual percentage of your shrinkage?

_____

_____

_____

Do you have the right policies and procedures that prevent shrinkage?

_____

_____

_____

How to Prevent Employee Theft

Why is it important for you to bring employee theft in your store under control?

The reason is this:

Employee theft is the number two source of retail shrinkage in many parts of the world. In fact, in the US, Canada and Australia, it is the leading cause of retail shrinkage.

Employee theft accounts for 35.3% of global retail shrinkage, while in the US it accounts for 43.7%.

The average cost of employee theft in a supermarket is $93,000 and approximately $243,000 to a hypermarket annually.

Taking advantage of their positions (access to security information, keys and security codes etc.), dishonest retail employees are capable of inflicting more damage on you than shoplifters. The average customer related theft costs you £66, while the average employee theft is estimated to cost you £1,318.

Due to their proximity to the system, employee theft is difficult to detect. It takes an average of 18 months to detect a retail employee theft.

Most instances of employee theft go undetected for years, especially if the individual involved is a store manager or in a senior management position.

So Why do Retail Employees Steal?

Rd. Donald R. Cressey "Fraud Triangle" theory revealed three factors that explain employee theft:

- The individual's financial situation
- The opportunity
- Their ability to justify their actions

How Does Employee Theft Take Place in a Retail Store?

OPPORTUNITY

If merchandise is placed in inadequately secured locations for example, high value items placed in warehouses without locks, merchandise not strategically placed on the shop floor, placed close to an exit or positioned in a place that facilitates easy removal from the store.

PERCEPTION

If employees perceive the consequences to be less severe to dissuade them from carrying out the act.

BENEFIT

If the benefit from stealing the merchandise outweighs the perceived cost of being caught, they will be willing to take the risk.

RATIONALE

If they rationalise their decision by saying something like "I am not paid enough for the work I am doing", "the organisation is rich therefore will not be affected by this or what everyone else is doing it anyway".

The above demonstrates that "opportunity" is the main reason employees steal.

The organization involved might not have the appropriate policies and procedures in place to limit the occurrences of theft.

For example, in many retail warehouses, high-value items are left lying around without any form of security.

Furthermore, newly hired employees are not given clear and concise policies and procedures regarding employee theft. The lack of policies and procedures and inadequate security of goods (especially high value items), sends a signal to employees that no one cares.

However, there is one very important aspect of opportunity that has repeatedly been ignored by many writers on the subject of employee theft.

They have mostly placed the onus on the employees or have presented the employees as antagonists who are disloyal to their employers.

Furthermore, when the issue of opportunity is discussed, it is done in terms of location of goods not in terms of organizational structure.

When I talk of opportunity in this sense, I mean the systems within the organizations that allow the theft to occur in the first instant.

When an employee notices that there are no coherent policies and procedures and top management have not demonstrated core values that others within the organization are expected to aspire to, then they have no reason to be loyal to the organization.

What are the Tell tail Signs of Employee Theft?

PRODUCT THEFT

SITUATION
- An employee hides or takes products without paying

WARNING SIGNS:
- A preference to park his/her car behind the store or next to the outside bins
- Seldom takes breaks with colleagues.
- Bagged merchandise stacked next to the till
- Stashing away goods in the store
- Shows a preference for inappropriately large workbags
- Always first in and last to leave
- Taking goods to and from toilets or changing room
- Product or packaging found in the vicinity of bins or compactors
- Discarded empty product packages found in warehouse or areas of assignment
- An eagerness to take out rubbish, especially just before a break or home time

NON SCANNING

SITUATION

- Cashier regularly marks down selling prices without authorisation

WARNING SIGNS:

- A price discrepancy as multiple items not scanned at the same price
- Cashier who manually enters price instead of scans items
- Cashier who has access to spare barcodes at the till
- Cashier with a below average customer spend for all periods
- Items on till records do not tally with the items covered in the transaction

EMPLOYEE STEALING CASH

SITUATION
- An employee steals cash

WARNING SIGNS:
- Above normal use of the 'no-sales' key
- Use of calculator or other counting aids to track cash removed.
- Frequent refunds
- Employee who regularly borrows money from colleagues
- Habitually closes tills or cashes up early.
- Till open for long periods after transactions
- Cash drawer remains open from one sale to the next
- Cashier holds on to cash and puts it aside instead of in the till
- Regularly adding vouchers to the till.

FRAUDULENT REFUNDS

SITUATION
- A customer service employee creates a false refund and takes the equivalent in cash from the till.

WARNING SIGNS:
- Receipt not given to customer resulting in customer complaint
- Customer receipts found on customer service counter or in the bin
- Processes a refund with a colleague's log on code
- Processes a fictitious refund with no customer present
- Processes a refund for an accomplice without returning merchandise
- Failing to issue customer receipts
- Falsified customer details on refund records

COLLUDING WITH SHOPLIFTERS

SITUATION

- An employee colludes with shoplifters and alerts them of loss prevention activities

WARNING SIGNS:

- Employee supplying customers with extra carrier bags
- Employee receiving lots of visitors during working hours
- Employee who unusually avoids management
- Employee monitoring the movements of loss prevention personnel or other store employees
- Employee who strikes up friendships with loss prevention or security officers

FALSIFIED VOIDS

SITUATION
- a) Cashier annuls a valid transaction and takes the equivalent in cash
- b) Cashier conspires to void items after they are scanned to reduce the actual amount to be paid

WARNING SIGNS:
- Annulled sales is followed by no-sale
- Multiple negative transactions
- Supervisors manually register a transaction sale or sanction person-al voids
- Customer receipts from that day discovered at the till or in bin next to cashier
- Cashier registers sizable overcharges repeatedly
- Cashiers with exceptionally low scanning average
- Cashiers failing to issue customer receipts
- Signs of calculating aids (i.e. paper/pencil, calculator, paper clips)

CASH OFFICE FRAUD

SITUATION

- a) A cash office employee fakes accounting figures thus enabling the removal of cash
- b) A cash office employee falsifies payroll or time sheets

WARNING SIGNS:

- Abnormal cash discrepancy
- Cash shortages discovered following audits of safe/petty cash
- Statements from the bank do not correspond with store deposit records
- Totals from cash office are out in sync with figures from bank deposits
- Your bank says deposit is short

CREDIT/DEBIT CARD FRAUD

SITUATION
- a) Cashier deliberately processes a stolen credit card as payment
- b) An employee refunds to their own or an accomplice's account

WARNING SIGNS:
- Employee records a customer's credit/debit card number
- Employee retains the customer's copy of a credit card receipt
- Differences in cash and credit totals
- Employee takes card away from the presence of the customer

MOST COMMON SIGNS TO LOOK OUT FOR

GENERAL SITUATION

- Retailers need to be mindful of the below signs which may signal theft in their store.

WARNING SIGNS:

- Employee who is extremely friendly with loss prevention personnel – he/she maybe monitoring their activities
- Employee constantly at odds with company's policies and procedures – discontented with superior
- Employee who doesn't take part in activities with other staff members
- Increase in variants prior to an employee holiday
- Employee who is always absent during audit and impedes audit of financial records

How to Prevent Employee Theft

There are two effective measures for, preventing employee theft.

These are:

- Intangible measure
- Tangible measures

INTANGIBLE

We read many books and conduct hours of internet research prior to writing this workbook.

The single theme that ran concurrently throughout all of the material was that employees who stole from their employers were disloyal criminals.

While it is true that stealing for whatever reason cannot be justified, it is important that we put the issue into proper perspective.

In their book 'Built to Last', authors Jim Collins and Jerry I Porras made an important point about the key ingredient required to building a great company.

One of those ingredients is "purpose beyond making money and core values".

They stated that all of the companies that are built to last are those with operational practices, which are in congruence with their core values.

Those values are communicated through the blood stream of the organisation from the CEO to the cleaner.

They live and breathe those values in their daily activities.

Another vital ingredient for creating greatness is creating a culture of discipline…where disciplined people take disciplined actions without the need for hierarchy.

When an organisation has a culture of discipline, people are willing to perform their duties independent of top management directives.

During a training session for some retail executives from the Middle East, I mentioned to my trainees that one of the most effective tools for preventing employee theft was to incentivise them.

One of the delegates responded to this suggestion by saying employees were being paid for a job therefore he saw no reason for incentivising them.

To an extent, he was right, yet the fact of the matter is every employee is a volunteer.

Whether they are paid or not, they volunteer their time and a piece of their lives working for an organisation.

They could choose to work for another organisation but they chose your organisation, therefore they deserve to be treated with respect.

How do you show them respect?

You do so by demonstrating genuine appreciation for their work.

You treat them like people not numbers and you genuinely care for them.

My trainee works for an organisation that has introduced the concept of "Saudinisation", however, almost all of their store managers are foreign.

What would motivate a Saudi to work and see a future in this company when most of the senior management is foreign?

If the company introduced a program in which foreigners are brought in to train Saudis to take over from them in a few years, it is only at that point there will be an alignment between what is being pronounced and what is actually practiced.

Like my Saudi friends, in many retail organisations, there is no alignment between what is written in the staff handbook and what is actually being practiced in the stores.

Employees do not see senior management as people who have their interest at heart therefore; they see no reason to be loyal to them.

The mentality in many retail organisations is that of a mini tyrant leading a group of worker bees, who are supposed to be at their beck and call.

When I was preparing this workbook, I researched the reason Tesco was in trouble.

One of the ex-senior executives said to a journalist, they treated staff with contempt.

I will not use those words but Tesco managers are under constant pressure to produce. It seems all top management does is pile pressure on them, and there is only so much pressure you can pile on people before they crack and stop thinking.

If Tesco wants to come back to profitability, they first need to change their attitude towards their managers.

In the sections on store design and visual merchandise display, I emphasize the fact that people buy emotionally but justify their decisions logically.

Your employees are emotional beings; they have similar emotional issues like your customers. You cannot ignore that in your dealings with your staff.

They are human beings. When they return home, they have wives, husbands, children, brothers and sisters like the rest of us.

Therefore, they deal with the same issues in their lives like the rest of humanity.

So if you need their loyalty and cooperation you need to make them feel that you understand the fact that they are human.

Most importantly, *if you want your employees to treat your customers with respect, you need to set an example by treating your employees with respect.*

TANGIBLE PREVENTION

1. Have a robust recruitment process

By having a robust recruitment process that involves:

- Pre-employment screening,
- Proper background/credit checks
- Thorough examination of past employment history/ references,

It is quite possible you can avoid recruiting the thief in the first instant.

2. Employee Theft Policies and Procedures

The following policies and procedures are essential for reducing employee theft:

- Proper Key and Access Code Management
- Scanning, Void, No-Sale Policies
- Employee Shopping Policy
- Markdowns Policy
- Receiving Policy

PERIODIC AND RANDOM AUDIT

- Shrinkage audit
- Inventory audit
- Purchase audit

SHIFT ROTATION AND MANDATORY HOLIDAYS

Many instances of employee theft go undetected for months, even years, because employees' knowledge of the organization's system gives them the ability to cover their tracks.

Therefore, staff shift, partner rotation makes it possible for other staff members to detect fraudulent activities.

Employees who fail to take their statutory holiday need to be of concern to retailers, this could be an indication that they are trying to conceal something.

It is incumbent upon retailers to ensure their employees use their holiday entitlements.

Not only is it good for their productivity but the absence of a staff member could result in some very interesting revelations about their activities on the job.

Workshop

Do you know the source of your employee theft?

_____

_____

_____

What policies and procedures do you have in place to prevent employee theft?

_____

_____

_____

How do you secure products in the backroom?

_____

_____

_____

Do you have adequate key control?

_____

_____

_____

How to Prevent Retail Employee Error

The issue of employee error has never been on the radar of loss prevention experts when devising policies and procedures for loss prevention (retail profit protection).

Most of the concentration has focused on employee or customer related theft and fraud.

This approach to loss prevention in many retail organizations has allowed employee errors to go on unnoticed and unabated.

Furthermore, even when the issue is discussed, the focus is primarily on simple errors such as pricing, administration or accounting.

Very little, if any, attention is paid to merchandising, procurement or procedural errors that are actually responsible for a larger percentage of losses within retail organizations.

I stumbled upon an interesting insight during one of our training sessions.

Addressing the subject of employee error, one of the delegates said he believed there was an important aspect of employee error that I had omitted, which was procurement error.

He went on to explain that in his organization, supplies are usually distributed amongst stores.

However because most of the purchasing decisions are based purely on price, the procurement department ends up purchasing surplus merchandise for stores that do not require the amount of stock that was shipped to them.

For example, they could purchase a large quantity of rice, because vendors offer them a special discount for purchasing a certain quantity.

While this may seem sensible on the surface, in practice much of the rice ends up staying in the warehouse until it decays and is thrown away.

Sometimes large amounts of rice are shipped to stores with the wrong demographics population that consumed less rice than they think.

This is because procurement works independently of the store management.

Purchasing decisions are not based upon previous transactional records of the stores; their focus is solely on getting the best deal from the supplier.

This approach ends up creating avoidable losses to the company.

This is particularly common in clothing stores where buyers purchase large amounts of a particular line hoping that it would rush off the shelves; yet by the end of the season, the clothes are still stacked somewhere in the warehouse.

The first step retailers must take to address employee error is to acknowledge the cost of it to their organization and pinpoint the particular areas where it occurs to enable them to be reduced.

This does not have to be a costly task; by implementing the appropriate policies and procedures employee errors can be prevented and minimized considerably.

It is not the cost of an error that retailers need to focus on, instead the focus should be on the amount it cost to rectify that error.

An 18% error cost (which is £36,000 for a store with a £10 million turnover) might appear insignificant on the surface.

However, when you consider that it would require sales of £3.6 million to recover the £36,000 losses resulting from employee error, you will easily realize it is much more cost-effective to prevent the error in the first place.

To put this in perspective, simply consider the amount of time and money necessary to accumulate sales of £3.6 million (if shrinkage level is 2.6% and profit margin is 1).

What Is Retail Employee Error?

Retail employee error occurs as a result of pricing and accounting mistakes, unintentional damage and over- or under-ordering.

Examples of employee error could be a cashier ringing up the wrong item into the wrong department, inventory counting inaccuracies, or distribution error that results in shortage or surplus in some stores as well as receiving mistakes.

These can all be caused by individual mistakes or could be systemic. They could result from a disorganized warehouse, poor administrative practices, and a lack of training or simple procedural errors.

Eliminating errors is virtually impossible in any working environment.

Fast paced activities, constant employee turnover, low wages and lapses in adhering to procedures all help to increase the possibility of multiple employee errors.

However, with the creation of the appropriate policies and procedures, well-trained staff and introduction of adequate mechanisms for monitoring compliance, these errors can be drastically reduced.

Types of Employee Error

Procurement Error

A buyer orders more stock than is needed for a particular store

Effect:

- Over ordering causes unnecessary expiration of perishable goods, damage to products or tying down valuable capital that could be used to order additional products or expand the business

Solutions:

- Ordering must be made in conjunction with sales data and demographics
- Buyers must coordinate with store managers when choosing the types of products required for a particular store.
- Buyers must not solely focus on discount or percentage of saving they will make when ordering; they must consider the speed of sales and the logistics of warehousing the products.
- Senior management must hold buyers accountable for large errors in buying that cause the company to lose huge amounts of money.

Merchandising Error

Products not securely merchandised on the shop floor

> **Effect:**
>
> - When goods are not merchandised securely on the shop floor, it facilitates their easy removal from the store by either shoplifters or dishonest employees.
> - Failing to secure goods on the shop floor sends a signal to shoplifters and dishonest employees alike that the company does not take the issue of loss prevention seriously.
>
> **Solutions:**
>
> - Involve store manager in the selection of location for merchandising of goods on the shop floor.
> - Involve the loss prevention department when making decisions on merchandising of goods in the store
> - Store design must take into account stock vulnerability and blind spots.
> - Take the appropriate precautions to ensure store design does not impede security.

Receiving Error

Failure to maximise supplier credit opportunity

Effect:

- In the contractual agreements between suppliers and retail organisations, there is always stipulation for credit, for products that are damaged or expired.

However, it is the receiver's responsibility to request such credits, as vendors would not voluntarily take back stock that is damaged or expired or offer stores credit.

- Furthermore, like the refund procedures of the stores themselves, suppliers have their own returns procedures.

So it is incumbent upon store managers to ensure that they train their staff to follow the vendor return procedures.

Solutions:

- Designated receiving employees need to be properly trained on the appropriate ways of requesting credit from suppliers.
- Create a mechanism for monitoring compliance with supplier credit procedures
- Ensure the procedure is organised and is carried on at a particular time every week
- Ensure all internal documentation reflects the inventory variations

Sales Floor Error

Pricing error

Effect:

- Inaccurate pricing is another major employee error. Inaccurate low price errors can cause losses to the retailer; however, inaccurate high pricing error can cause customer dissatisfaction.

- Pricing errors usually occur during promotional or sales periods. If changes are made during one shift and the information is not transmitted to the next shift, it can result in avoidable errors.

Solutions:

- Train a designated scan file maintenance coordinator.

- Designated scanning coordinator and department managers must be held accountable for pricing errors.

- Regularly check, compare and verify as necessary all prices on the sales floor to ensure accuracy.

Sales Floor Error

Failure to record damaged or distressed stock

Effect:

- When damaged or distressed goods are discarded without a proper mechanism for accountability and adjustment of inventory records, it results in artificial inventory inaccuracy.

Solutions:

- Train employees to be honest and open about damaged products to ensure that they report it to their supervisors or line manager without fear of sanction
- Ensure damaged or distressed goods are returned to suppliers for credit
- Create a log book in which all damaged and distressed goods are logged and investigated to prevent future occurrence
- Discounting and bulk selling damaged and distressed goods can minimise loss

Sales Floor Error

Lack of proper mechanism for product rotation

> **Effect:**
> - The lack of adequate mechanisms for ensuring proper product rotation results in unnecessary wastage and product expiration
>
> **Solutions:**
> - Install mechanisms for accountability for product rotation
> - Maintain constant vigil and ensure short shelf life products are managed to prevent expiration
> - Product rotation has to be included as a daily task and specific individuals have to be assigned to it each day.
> - Ensure products are discounted before their expiration date.
> - Managers and supervisors, on their store walk must pay particular attention to perishable products to ensure that the appropriate discounts are applied.

Sales Floor Error

Damage caused by customer or shelf fillers

Effect:

- When products are damaged or distressed by customers or employees filling shelves they should be discounted or discarded.

Solutions:

- Products on a shelf should never exceed a certain height
- Shelf fillers must be trained in the correct handling of sharp tools used to open packages and crates.
- Regularly, face up products to avoid situations in which customers have to struggle to reach them, resulting in breakage
- Stock cages must be attended at all times, especially when customers are in the store.
- Products have to be properly arranged by order pickers, placing fragile objects in their own cages and ensuring heavier items are placed at the bottom
- Order pickers must properly label fragile products to make it easy for shelf fillers to recognise them
- Products must be prearranged in the warehouse before being moved to the shop floor

Sales Floor Error

Causing risk of injury to customers during shelf filling

> **Effect:**
>
> - Customers injured as a result of a cage or trolley used for shelf filling can result in costly injury claims.
>
> **Solutions:**
>
> - Shelves should be stacked to a specified limit
> - All sharp tools must be carefully handled during replenishment
> - Never, leave stock unattended on the shop floor
> - Regularly face-up stock during the day

Sales Floor Error

Failing to notice large gaps in display shelf

Effect:

- A large gap in display shelf is an indication of shoplifting or inventory shortage.
- This could result in inventory inaccuracy or customer dissatisfaction

Solutions:

- When a large gap is noticed in the shelf display, an immediate investigation needs to be launched to ascertain the reason for it
- Check inventory and sales records and make comparisons
- Keep a constant vigil on all high value items and high-risk areas
- Train store associates to recognise large gaps in shelf display and immediately report their findings to management

Sales Floor Error

Employees use stock for store operations

Effect:

- The use of inventory for store operation results in shrinkage. While this may seem harmless, if stock taken from store inventory are not properly recorded, it can lead to inventory shortage.

Solutions:

- Whenever store inventory is used for operational purposes, a proper record must be kept and all inventory records must be adjusted to reflect the new inventory position.

- Only permit supervisors and managers to remove inventory for store operations

Administrative Error

Inefficient procedures for managing the movement of money around the store

Effect:
- Inadequate money movement management creates exposure to robbery and temptation for dishonest employees

Solutions:
- Never leave the till draw open after a transaction
- Ensure the till is neatly arranged separating cash from other forms of payment
- Keep accurate records of all cash pick-ups
- Set up an alert system that spots large cash build-ups and automatically calls for pick-up
- Cashiers should be held accountable for all variances in cash.
- Cashiers needs to be trained in the correct procedure for requesting cash pick-ups

Cashier Error

Accepting counterfeit money

Effect:

- Valueless notes in the till

Solutions:

- Implement a procedure for cashiers to alert management whenever they receive counterfeit notes.
- Display procedure close to the till facing the cashier with a diagram.
- Train cashiers in the use of counterfeit identification pens and other security devices that detect counterfeit notes.

Cashier Error

Blind scanning of items, cashier passing products through the till without checking the price

> **Effect:**
> - Due to the fact that most tills in retail stores scan automatically, many cashiers fail to check the products they are scanning.
> - Cashiers need to be aware of current prices of products in the store so that in the event a customer swaps the sticker, they will be alerted to it.
>
> **Solutions:**
> - Cashiers must be constantly made aware of changes in prices of products in the store, especially promotional items
> - Train cashiers to look at product prices as they walk through the different aisles
> - Ensure cashiers are made aware of high theft or high value items to enable them to be vigilant when ringing in such items.

Administrative Error

Promotional items not properly communicated to cashier

> **Effect:**
> - Misunderstanding of promotional items can result in a customer services nightmare.
>
> **Solutions:**
> - Program tills to identify multiple promotional sales
> - Brief cashiers on promotions and new ringing sequences at the start of their shift
> - Retrain cashiers to ring promotional items correctly.

Cashier Error

Cashier incorrectly packs customer shopping

> **Effect:**
> - Damages resulting from improper packing by the cashier causes shrinkage as the store will be forced to replace the items
>
> **Solutions:**
> - Train cashiers to properly handle fragile products
> - Train cashiers in the best procedures to pack products safely

Cashier Error

Cashier inadvertently processes sales from one department into another

> **Effect:**
> - When the wrong product is scanned into the wrong department, it causes artificial shortage in one department and credit for another department
>
> **Solutions:**
> - Train cashiers to scan products into the right departments
> - Confirm that information in the master register matches department information

Cashier Error

Irregular use of multiple items key

> **Effect:**
> - This could result in expensive products being processed as low value items
> - Errors could be compounded.
> - This could affect inventory accuracy
>
> **Solutions:**
> - Require cashiers to scan items individually
> - Train cashiers at regular intervals
> - Regularly check cashiers scanning percentage to highlight training requirements, any issues or faulty equipment

Cashier Error

Cashier unaware of an item's price decides to make a guess

Effect:

- This may result in shrinkage as cashier may charge lower to prevent conflict with a customer.

Solutions:

- Train cashiers to identify products
- Constantly check cashiers to ensure they are up to speed with scanning policies and procedures
- Never permit cashiers to guess prices
- Ensure quick price check system is in place
- Set up a clear and visible support system to help cashiers identify items

Cashier Error

Failing to correct scanning errors

Effect:
- Cashiers display an unwillingness to delay customers or hold up their till queue.
- Untrained supervisors are unable to attend to cashier errors
- Cashiers may leave such errors uncorrected or try to hide them

Solutions:
- Develop an error alert system in which cashiers are instructed to call in supervisors as soon as an error is detected so that errors are addressed and corrected with minimal delay
- Provide cashiers with adequate training
- Train supervisors in the most basic correction procedures to prevent long queues and shrinkage

Cashier Error

Incorrect use of scales

Effect:
- Inaccurate scales may register higher or lower weight

Solutions:
- Train cashiers to use scales correctly
- Calibrate scales daily to ensure accuracy

Backroom Error

Stock damage

Effect:
- Damaged products lose part or all of their value

Solutions:
- Keep stock level in the warehouse as low as possible
- Keep busy areas of the stockroom clear of any obstruction
- Keep the stockroom tidy and organised
- Provide warehouse staff with adequate training
- Secure all high value items in secure locations in the storeroom

Backroom Error

Products disappear in warehouse

Effect:
- Lost product results in inadequate inventory, over ordering and a waste of time trying to locate it

Solutions:
- Manage stock levels to ensure sufficient stock to satisfy customer demand
- Keep stockroom tidy and organised
- Keep stock level in the warehouse as low as possible

Backroom Error

Product is mistakenly thrown into the compactor

Effect:
- When a warehouse is untidy, there is a possibility of good products being mistakenly thrown into the compactor resulting in preventable shrinkage

Solutions:
- Ensure compactor is used by only designated employees
- Ensure the compactor is locked at all times when not in use
- Maintain tidiness in the warehouse
- Keep the compacter far from the warehouse
- Recycle all recyclable items

Auditing Error

Inventory miscount

Effect:
- Miscounted inventory creates a complete disorder in the organisation's inventory system, potentially resulting in shortages or surplus.

Solutions:
- Conduct inventory count at specific intervals
- Every effort must be made to ensure that all items are counted and that the count is accurate
- Do not add stock arriving during an inventory stock take to the count.

Ordering Error

Order picking error

Effect:
- Order picking error causes acute inventory inaccuracies as there might be adequate supply within the supply chain as a whole however, there might be shortages and surplus in some stores

Solutions:
- Train pickers to select products as accurately as possible
- Train pickers in product knowledge to ensure they are familiar with the products they are picking
- Use the latest technology to ensure accuracy of the process
- Assign accountability for error to supervisor and managers

How to Reduce Employee Error

Employee error can never be eliminated; however, it can be minimized through the implementation of the following measures.

Ensure employees:

- Receive thorough training for the job / tasks they are assigned to
- Understand the company's policies and procedures
- Are confident using the equipment
- Are issued with clearly defined job descriptions
- Regular oversight is also essential for monitoring employee's progress

Workshop

What is the cost of employee error to your organisation?

_____

_____

_____

What is the main cause of your employee error?

_____

_____

_____

What actions have you taken to reduce employee error?

_____

_____

_____

Do you have mechanisms for monitoring employee compliance to policies and procedures?

_____

_____

_____

How to Create An Efficient Receiving Process

The receiving process is unstructured in many retail organizations, with no written policies and procedures.

This results in receiving shrinkage, accounts for an estimated 10% of total retail shrinkage.

In an average supermarket, this amounts to £37,750.

Supply theft and vendor fraud are responsible for the majority of receiving shrinkage.

Receivers play a crucial role in every retail store.

They are the first line of defence through which every item must pass before entering the store's inventory system.

If the process and the individual lack integrity, this will have a negative ripple effect throughout the entire store's inventory system.

When suppliers notice that receivers are ignorant of the merchandise they are receiving, they are certain to exploit the situation by either short supplying or charging for undelivered goods.

For this reason, it is imperative that every retail organization have designated and well trained receivers who possess adequate knowledge of the products they are expected to receive and the technology they operate.

Below is a checklist for an effective receiving process

1. When preparing to receive goods, keep the warehouse clean and organised.
2. Rotate stock in the warehouse and move some to the shop floor as required.
3. Ensure extra staff are on hand to receive the goods.
4. Count the number of cages or pallets ensuring that where possible boxes are counted.
5. Inspect the consignment for damage, distress or leakage.
6. Record any shortage or surplus and ensure credit is requested from the supplier.
7. Rotate receivers to prevent collusion with suppliers.

Causes of Receiving Shrinkage
Vendor Theft & Fraud

Vendor dishonesty can occur in many ways including:

- Supplying fewer products than charged for.
- Manipulation of credit to avoid buying back expired stock.
- Inaccurate invoicing.
- Supplying nearly expired merchandise but charging full price.
- Partial delivery of merchandise.
- Fiddling with merchandise to be credited.

The Supply Chain Dilemma

The benchmark of success for most retail internal distribution systems is product flow rather than loss prevention or shrinkage management.

The basic logic behind this approach is twofold:

First and foremost, to prevent the expiration of goods in the warehouse.

Secondly, the books of the organization as a whole need to remain balanced, despite overages or shortages within individual store.

Tesco is a prime example of this scenario.

When goods are received in a Tesco store, there is either a shortage or an overage for the particular store.

The company's perception is that as long as the products exist within Tesco's supply chain network, they are not counted as shrinkage.

There are two major problems with this arrangement; it encourages dishonesty within the supply chain and it also causes significant shrinkage.

Additionally, if there is constant overage in stores, this will clearly result in stores receiving products they do not require.

Another principle omitted from supply chain relationships is the fundamental principle that states, *"If the customer has not bought, no one has sold"*.

Goods sitting in the regional or shop warehouse are a monetary liability until they are moved to the shop floor or placed in the customers' shopping baskets.

In order for a supply chain system to be effective, mechanisms must be employed for performance measurement.

The key performance indicator should be the reliability of the supplier; if a supplier delivers an order late it can cause shortage, ultimately causing customer service problems for the store.

Reliability is measured by assessing the price of the system that is affected because of the delayed delivery, multiplied by the number of days or hours it is late.

Applying a monetary value to this situation enables suppliers to see the cost implications their actions have on the company, thereby forcing them to take corrective action to ensure deliveries arrive on time.

When goods arrive at the store, receivers must record any discrepancies discovered between the goods delivered and those stated on the delivery note.

If any item is found as part of the stock but not recorded in the delivery notes, the following actions are advisable:

1. Isolate those items from the rest of the delivery.
2. Inform the distribution centre immediately.
3. The receiver must either log in the items in his store or forward it to another store.
4. Ensure all records are adjusted to reflect the new inventory status.

How to Train Receiving Employees

Receiving is the first line of defence in any retail environment.

Backdoor receivers literally hold the chequebook of that organization. Therefore, it is crucial to a retail business that these individuals receive a high level of training.

Receiver training must include the following areas:

1. Merchandise/product knowledge.
2. Basic mathematics to enable them to properly calculate.
3. The use of automated systems.
4. Store credit monitoring.

How to Prevent Receiving Losses

Effective prevention and/or reduction of receiving shrinkage requires the implementation of the following strategies:

1. Authorised Key Control
2. Receiver Training
3. Clearly Written Policies and Procedures
4. Effective Use of Technology
5. Warehouse Stock Control

Workshop

What is the main cause of your receiving shrinkage?

_____

_____

_____

What are you doing to prevent vendor theft and fraud in your store?

_____

_____

_____

What measures do your take to limit supply chain mistakes?

_____

_____

_____

Do you have trained receiving staff?

_____

_____

_____

What technology do you use to improve your replenishment process?

_____

_____

_____

Perishable and Non-Perishable Shrinkage

Visit any large supermarket in the morning the aroma in the air is always that of freshly baked bread.

The reason for this is; customers will frequent a particular supermarket for its perishable department. Therefore it is vital that freshness becomes the operating philosophy of any retail organisation that wants to remain profitable.

A produce department accurately merchandised is a sight to behold; it is a symbol of beauty and magnificence.

It conveys a message of freshness to customers, which in turn creates customer loyalty and develops a satisfying perception about the supermarket.

The perishable department distinguishes one supermarket from another.

Product availability, freshness and quality contribute to the competitive edge one supermarket, has over another.

It is estimated that customers will spend 8% of their grocery outgoings in a store they perceive to have fresh produce.

Four essential facts about the perishable department:

1. It drives sales and profit.
2. Stores lose 20% of available perishable profit to shrinkage.
3. Reducing perishable shrinkage by 20% will increase total store profit by 33%.
4. Perishable department contributes the highest income; ironically it is also responsible for the highest level of shrinkage

Causes of Perishable Shrinkage

- Cashier Mistakes (15%): 15% of store shrinkage is due to cashier errors. You can sort this by compliance testing, policies & procedures, and auditing.
- Incorrect Handling (21%): Train your staff in correct handling procedures and you can significantly reduce this aspect of your shrinkage.
- Insufficient Ordering (27%): By following 'smart ordering' and ordering for three days, your ordering process can become efficient.
- Spoilage (21%): You will inevitable have far less spoilage and discarded products if you adhered to proper ordering and handling practices.
- Delivery Distress (4%): This is slightly more difficult to control as sometimes products in transit unavoidably get damaged.
- Inadequate Admin (12%): Adhering to proper file management policies and procedures will reduce your shrinkage.

56% of total store shrinkage comes from meat, produce, deli, seafood, floral and bakery.

- These same departments contribute 30% of total store sales.

15% of total store shrinkage comes from the produce department.

- 9.1% of a typical supermarket sales comes are from the produce department & produce department shrinkage rate is 5.40% of retail sales.

What Causes Perishable Shrinkage

- Product receiving and handling practices
- Spoilage due to over stacking products
- Mistakes allowing stock to overstay in the backroom
- Theft by customers and employees

The Ultimate Challenge is to determine the amount required for maximum sales and minimum waste. This is a delicate balance to strike at all times.

How to Prevent Perishable Shrinkage

- Correct Handling
- Order for 3 days
- Smart Display Space Allocation
- Focus On Customer Demand
- Sell Rather Than Lose
- Cashier Awareness
- Code Storage Chiller
- Order Smart
- Refrigeration Blinds
- Open Products at The Right Time

Workshop

Do you have an efficient product receiving and handling process in your store?

_____

_____

_____

What do you do to prevent spoilage due to over stocking of products?

_____

_____

_____

How do you ensure stock is not left to expire in the backroom?

_____

_____

_____

What measure do you have in place to prevent theft either by customers or by employees?

_____

_____

_____

Non-Perishable Shrinkage

Non-perishable goods, such as groceries, health & beauty items and general merchandise, make up about 60% of a store's sales.

Damage, theft and accidents are the most notable causes of non-perishable shrinkage.

Non-perishable shrinkage can be classified as known and unknown.

Non-perishable shrinkage is easier to control than perishable shrinkage, with the implementation of a number of policies and procedures.

Classification of Non-Perishable Shrinkage

Known Shrinkage

The source for known shrinkage can be easily pinpointed. It's the result of damaged goods, administrative errors or fraud.

Unknown Shrinkage

Unknown shrinkage is a loss that cannot be pinpointed at the time of occurrence.

Incidents of theft, whether customer or employee related, can cause unknown shrinkage.

The reason for unknown shrinkage is the amount of time it takes to detect.

It could take weeks or even months before the problem is discovered.

This is especially true in stores that do not have a good inventory management system.

Non-Perishable shrinkage occurs in the following departments:

- Grocery
- General Merchandise
- Health & Beauty

Examples of causes of such shrinkage are:

- Damage
- Accident
- Theft

Breakdown of Non-Perishable Shrinkage

- Grocery: 56%
- General Merchandise: 19%
- Health & Beauty: 13%
- Beer, Wine, and Spirit: 4%
- Frozen Food: 3%
- Other: 4%

Strategies for Preventing Non-Perishable Shrinkage

Preventing non-perishable shrinkage is a straightforward task in comparison to perishable shrinkage.

What is required is the introduction of the correct policies and procedures, the training of staff to implement those policies and procedures and the installation of mechanisms for monitoring compliance.

The process needs to take the following format:

1. Controlling Known Loss

Controlling known loss, requires establishing mechanisms to ensure proper records are kept of all customer returns, damaged, distressed or expired goods.

2. Backdoor Receiving

A majority of store deliveries come from their own warehouses and suppliers deliver the remainder to the store.

Since receiving shrinkage accounts for approximately 10% of retail shrinkage, it is imperative that the receiving process is diligently overseen.

3. Pricing Management

When addressing pricing discrepancies in the store, take the following into consideration:

1. Procedures for pricing change
2. Management of pricing/scan information
3. Auditing of direct supplier pricing
4. Warehouse Inventory Control

Retailers have one thing in common, irrespective of size, the issue of forecasting.

Retailers have yet to find a fail-safe way to forecast customer's behaviour.

Software is available to help retailers make an educated guess, although it is not 100% accurate.

The inability to forecast has been responsible for either over-ordering or out-of-stock scenarios in many retail stores.

One way to limit this problem is to organise your warehouse.

Workshop

What is the main cause of your shrinkage: Damage, theft or accident?

_____

_____

_____

What measures do you have in place to reduce each of the above causes of your shrinkage?

_____

_____

_____

How often do you conduct inventory control?

_____

_____

_____

Is your inventory control conducted by internal or external staff or both?

How organised is your warehouse?

How to Prevent Shoplifting

Why do you need to prevent shoplifting from your store?

Shoplifting is no longer a simplistic and petty teenage criminal, nor is it carried out exclusively by the homeless and addicts.

Shoplifting has evolved to the more professional level of Organized Retail Crime (ORC).

Presently, it is a well-known fact that the ORC is directly responsible for the majority of items stolen from retailers worldwide.

Thus, it is also no surprise that the sophistication involved in the act of shoplifting is on the rise to levels the retail industry never thought conceivable.

These mastermind groups consist of highly trained individuals performing acts of thievery with an air of professionalism that is downright amazing.

While you can still point to transients, teenagers and young adults as common culprits behind shoplifting, the reality is that the ORC nets a far bigger piece of the pie.

The internet has produced some great websites for trading and selling in the 21st century, including sites like eBay and Craig List.

Such websites have introduced a completely new dynamic to the shopping industry – and a whole new dynamic to retail crime.

ORC criminal gangs love to target retail organizations that they view as easy or soft targets.

These are the stores that prefer to focus on quality customer service, displaying their merchandise in a manner that is vulnerable to theft – making it easy to be removed from the store.

With the exception of the US, Canada, and Australia, shoplifting continues to be the number one cause of retail shrinkage in all corners of the world.

Why Does Shoplifting Take Place?

The simple answer to this question is because shoplifters can get away with it.

Shoplifting is a crime of opportunity, when you remove the opportunity you remove the possibility.

Two things continue to hinder retailers' effort to fight shoplifting:

1. The continuous implementation of the wrong strategies
2. Their unwillingness to create and implement the necessary policies and procedures required to prevent shoplifting in their stores.

Retailers worldwide spend billions on loss prevention technology, yet never examine the needed changes to policies and procedures to prevent shoplifting from flourishing.

Organised Retail Crime (ORC): The New Dynamic in Shoplifting

The emergence of Organized Retail Crime (ORC) into the world of shoplifting has introduced a completely new dynamic to the retail industry.

Traditionally, shoplifting has been committed by individuals seeking survival, personal gain, or support of their habit.

Interestingly enough, members of these organized criminal gangs do not fit these descriptions.

Rather, they are gangs of well-organized, professional thieves who exhibit a level of sophistication never before witnessed in the retail industry.

ORC costs retailers millions annually with no signs of slowing down.

For example, a BBC report on ORC published on 11 January 2010 (Crime gangs 'dominate shop theft') illustrates the level of damage ORC is capable of inflicting on a retail store.

They are capable of stealing up to £7,500 worth of products within 4 minutes and almost £100,000 worth of merchandise daily.

When you consider their operational sophistication, meticulous planning, and capability of walking away with thousands of pounds in merchandise, the ORC is truly a very real force to be reckoned with.

The primary gang active in the UK is the 150 member strong Glasgow-based McGovern team.

This gang has terrorized Scotland for many years, and is now branching out all over the UK.

It is conceivable that they are even spreading their reach into Europe.

The most lethal ORC gangs can be found in the former eastern blocks as well as in the republics that comprised the former Yugoslavia.

Thousands of members strong, these gangs routinely hit retailers they perceive to be easy targets around Europe.

Due to the ease of international travel in the EU, these individuals can very quickly and easily migrate from country to country, perpetrating their crimes.

What's more, these gangs make use of fake and stolen credit/debit cards that they are able to use for ordering thousands of pounds of merchandise to false addresses, taking the merchandise and disappearing into thin air.

Hot Spots

The figure below shows the most frequently target departments: Health & beauty followed by meat, baby products, cigarettes, beer, wine & spirit.

- Health & Beauty: 32%
- Meat: 24%
- Cigarettes: 13%
- Baby Products: 13%
- Beer, Wine, and Spirits: 10%
- Other: 8%

Hot Products

> Below is the list of the most targeted products:
> - Health, Beauty and Cosmetic Items: 22%
> - Meat: 14%
> - Cigarettes: 14%
> - Baby Milk: 8%
> - Analgesics: 8%
> - Razor Blades: 8%
> - Batteries: 7%
> - Alcohol: 5%
> - Other: 14% (represents CD's, DVD's, and electronic devices)

The above figure shows the most frequently targeted products: Health, beauty & cosmetics, followed by meat & cigarettes, razor blades, analgesics and batteries.

DVDs, CDs and electronic devices are the products most at risk in department stores and superstores.

Shoplifting Techniques

- Pushchairs or car seats contained in shopping trolleys are often used to conceal stolen goods
- Shoplifters may snatch goods making a run for a waiting get-away vehicle.
- Some shoplifters wrap clothes around their legs, or tuck stolen items into socks.
- Female shoplifters may carry items between bras, hidden under long dresses, tights, or overcoats.
- In fitting rooms – they put on stolen clothes or shoes. They either abandon their own garments or put them back on to cover the stolen attire.
- They conceal stolen products in bags, newspapers, shopping bags, purses, clothes fitted with large pockets, inner lining of coats, or un-der clothing.
- Shoplifters operate solo or in a group. If functioning as a group, one individual is commonly employed to distract loss prevention personnel.

When loss prevention personnel target the person who seems to behave suspiciously, the accomplice fulfils his/her act un-noticed.

Tell-Tale Signs of a Shoplifter

- A group of teenagers entering a store at the same time, few of them will cause disturbance to draw attention away from the main person carrying on the stealing.
- Out of place outfits i.e. overcoat on a hot day or a raincoat when it is sunny
- Somebody carrying empty bags, boxes or umbrellas, which they can use to cover stolen items
- A worried-looking person who constantly touches the rear of his/her head, tugging at sleeves, or altering socks, breaks into cold sweat and blushing
- Incredibly picky individuals who are unable to decide on a purchase decision.
- Someone visiting the store repeatedly without buying anything.
- Someone placing his/her personal items in trolley
- Repeatedly looking around rather than at merchandise on the shelf or in their hands
- An empty shelf or hole in the shelf
- An early morning or late night shopper

How to Prevent Shoplifting

Shoplifting, like any crime, is impossible to eliminate.

For some people, shoplifting is a profession; this is how they make their living.

The perceived danger or difficulties they may encounter at a particular time are not enough to dissuade them from committing the crime.

Some also see shoplifting as literally their only means of survival.

For drug addicts wanting to feed their habits, shoplifting provides the only means of obtaining the necessary cash.

With this in mind, how can retailers prevent their store from being used by a professional shoplifter who sees it as a job or from drug addicts who consider it their cash dispenser?

The first step is to understand that shoplifters will operate in an environment they perceive as EASY.

Therefore, it is essential to ensure that your store is not perceived as an easy target.

In many instances, when a shoplifters take up residency in your store, they never leave until the final curtain is brought down.

These are some of the measures that can be used to help combat shoplifting:

- Change of Policies and Procedures
- Trained Employees
- Strategic Merchandising of Goods
- Use Preventative Store Design
- Use Excellent Customer Service
- Train Loss Prevention Personnel
- Use Specific Strategies for Stopping Organised Retail Crime

Workshop

Have you trained your employees in shoplifting prevention?

_____

_____

_____

Do you have a specific strategy in place for fighting Organised Retail Crime gangs?

_____

_____

_____

Do you deal with your shoplifting problems from the source: your policies and procedures?

_____

_____

_____

What technology do you use to prevent shoplifting from your store?

_____

_____

_____

Do you provide shoplifters the opportunity to steal from your store?

_____

_____

_____

Summary

I have made three basic premises, through this workbook.

Premise number one:

To increase retail sales you need a combination of:

- Good store design
- Attractive visual merchandise display

Good store design and attractive visual merchandise display serve four functions:

- Attract customers into your store
- Retain them in the store longer
- Persuade them to buy
- Automatically trigger repeat purchase

In order to achieve all of the above you need to answer these three questions:

- Who I am going to sell to
- What I am going to sell to them
- How I am going to sell it to them

Premise number two:

To increase retail sales without simultaneously increasing profit is false economy.

You will not remain solvent for a long time.

The simplest jolt in the economy and you are out of business.

To increase sales while simultaneously increasing profit, you need to increase sales and reduce shrinkage.

With an effective loss prevention strategy, you can reduce your shrinkage by 84%, which will result in a 51% profit increase.

Premise number three:

The third premise is, you cannot do the same thing and expect different result.

The retail industry needs to change if it wants meet the challenges of the new retail environment.

Tesco succeeded in becoming one of the most profitable retailers in the world and one of the most profitable businesses in the UK because it followed the principles I have outlined in this workbook.

Harrods remains the favourite shopping place of the rich and famous because it followed the principles outlined in this workbook.

Holland & Barrett is the second most profitable business in the UK because it followed the principles outlined in this workbook.

Richer Sound has the highest sales per sq. ft. than any other retailer in the world because it followed the principles outlined in this workbook.

What you have learnt from this workbook are principles, they are not techniques.

If you apply them you will succeed in your retail business, there are no two ways to it.

They have worked for countless successful retailers and they can work for you too if you put them to work in your business.

If you don't follow them, you will continue to struggle and eventually fail.

I hope you do.

Thanks for giving me the privilege to be of service to you.

Foot Note

As I was completing this workbook and my 'How to Increase Retail Sales' home study course, two things happened that might make some of the information in this workbook obsolete.

First, La Senza is back into administration.

The only comment I will make about that is: I said it.

When it was announced that La Senza, had come out of it first administration, I said it was impossible because they had not dealt with the underlying issues that sent the retailer into administration the first time.

Like many retail businesses that go in and out of administration, all the administrators did was find a buyer to pour lots of money into the brand the first few months, slice prices to attract customers, while neglecting to address the underlying issues that sent the business into administration.

It is tantamount to taking an old building with lots of structural defects, painting it and marketing it as a new building.

As long as the structural defects are not dealt with, the building remains an old building despite the new paint.

La Senza like many struggling retailers will continue to struggle until it address the root causes of its problems.

The second thing that has happened is Tesco CEO has been fired.

Can you imagine how I feel?

Really, really P off!

I am sure I am more P off than him.

The reason I am P off is I have built my entire marketing around his misery.

It's like a newspaper or TV station that builds its reputation on a single event or individual.

'Once upon a time, Tesco was the second most profitable retailer in the world, the fourth most profitable business in the UK.

At one point, for every twelve pounds spent in the UK, one pound was spent at Tesco.

At present Tesco is struggling to compete against the likes of Aldi and Lidl.

What is the reason for Tesco transformation from one of British greatest export to an ordinary retailers'?

Those are some of the questions I answered in this workbook and home study course.

I explained how Tesco became a retail giant and the reason for its current predicament.

I then provided advice on how the retailer can bounce back and show other retail organisation how to avoid similar fate.

Tesco being the central theme of my workbook and home study course, I built my entire marketing campaign around its current difficulties, which is the reason I am really, really P off with Tesco board for choosing now of all time to fire their CEO.

They should have at least waited until I launch my home study course…Dame it…

Now I have to think of a completely fresh approach to my marketing.

I will send a copy of this workbook to the new CEO and hope that he implement many of the ideas.

I will keep you posted on his reaction.

Great Books by Romeo

Book Romeo now!

+44 (0)20 8798 0579

romeo@theprofitexperts.co.uk

27.9% The Most Effective Retail Shrinkage Reduction Technologies

Prior to investing in any technology, there are vital questions that need to answered; those questions along with their answers can be found in this e-book.

This e-book was conceived out of our own desperate efforts to answer those questions.

What you will learn:

- Technologies That Prevent Employee Theft
- Technologies That Prevent Shoplifting
- Receiving Technologies
- Multi-purpose Technologies

12.24% The Most Effective Retail Employee Error Reduction Strategies

Employee errors in pricing, accounting and receiving contribute approximately 18% of retail shrinkage; this equates to £18,623 in losses to an average supermarket or store and almost £49,679 in losses to a superstore. This means that a store or supermarket that operates with a 1% net profit will need to make an additional £3million in annual sales in order to recover profit lost due to employee errors. By the same measure a typical hyper store will need to increase its sales by £8million.

You will learn:

- Constitutes as Retail Employee Error
- to Calculate the Cost of Employee Error
- to Calculate Additional Sales Required to Recover Losses Caused by Employee Error
- of Employee Error
- to Reduce Employee Error
- Ultimate Employee Error Prevention Formula
- to Apply the Lessons from This E-Book to Your Business

43.5% The Most Effective Retail Profit Protection Strategies

The retail landscape is changing rapidly with the constant increase in internet shopping. From 2005 to 2009, the online shopping population grew to 1.6 billion.

It is predicted to rise to 2.3 billion by 2014 with gross revenue totalling $778.6 billion. This is bad news for traditional brick and mortar retail businesses.

The question is: are you prepared? You will find your answer in this eBook.

What you will learn:

- The Conventional Approach to Loss prevention
- Why Loss Prevention is Critical to Retail
- Loss Prevention Spending vs Return on Investment
- What You Are Losing
- Profit vs Sales Calculation
- How to Create a Culture of Loss Prevention
- Effective Shrinkage Management Strategies
- The Ultimate Profit Protection Formula

24.5% The Most Effective Perishable And Non-Perishable Shrinkage Reduction Strategies

This e-book is jam packed with information on the causes of retail shrinkage, types of retail shrinkage, the cost of shrinkage to the retail industry and how shrinkage can be prevented. It is a comprehensive e-book on how and why shrinkage occurs and it provides a step-by-step guide on how to prevent shrinkage.

You will learn:

- An Introduction to Perishable Shrinkage
- Breakdown of Perishable Shrinkage
- Causes of Perishable Shrinkage
- How to Prevent Perishable Shrinkage
- The Ultimate Perishable Shrinkage Prevention Formula
- An Introduction to Non-Perishable Shrinkage
- Classification of Non-Perishable Shrinkage
- Breakdown of Non-Perishable Shrinkage
- Strategies for Preventing Non-Perishable Shrinkage
- The Ultimate Non-Perishable Shrinkage Prevention Formula
- How to Apply The Lessons From This E-Book to Your Business

27.8% The Most Effective Retail Employee Theft Reduction Strategies

The majority of retail employees are decent people who go to work each day to serve their customers and make their living.

However, there are the rotten apples that contaminate the good names of the rest.

This e-book is an instructional guide to retailers to show them how to minimise and prevent employee theft in their stores. Like shoplifting most incidents of employee theft occur because the opportunity exists. When retailers remove the opportunity, they can reduce the possibilities. This e-book will show retailers how to remove the opportunities that allow employee theft in their stores.

You will learn:

- Why Employees Steal
- The Process of Employee Theft
- Signs of Employee Theft
- How to Calculate the Cost of Employee Theft
- How to Prevent Employee Theft
- How Technology Can Help Prevent Employee Theft
- The Ultimate Employee Theft Prevention Formula

84%: The Most Effective Strategies for Increasing Retail Profit

The formula for increasing profit in retail is to increase sales and reduce shrinkage. How can retailers increase sales and reduce shrinkage? The answer is in this book.

You will learn everything you need to know about:

- Creating a Culture of Loss Prevention
- Employee Error
- Employee Theft
- Shoplifting
- Perishable and Non-Perishable Shrinkage
- Receiving Shrinkage
- Technologies that Help to Reduce Retail Shrinkage

Visual Merchandise: How to Create a Beautiful Yet Profitable Display

Merchandise display is the most effective form of advertising for a retail store. The more attractive a display, the higher the possibility of increasing sales. This book will show retailers how to create a display that is so attractive that it would increase their footfall tenfold.

You will learn:

- The psychology behind visual merchandising
- How to use visual merchandising to increase retail sales
- Challenges facing visual merchandisers
- How to burst the price myth with creative merchandise display
- The best merchandise display strategies
- How to maximise display space allocation with creative fixtures
- The pros and cons of using a planogram
- The pros and cons of hiring visual merchandising companies
- Most effective visual merchandise technologies
- How to display merchandise for maximum profit

Store Design Blueprint: How to Design an Attractive But Profitable Store

There are three fundamental principles that underpin a retail store design:

1. Attract customers as they pass by the store
2. Entice them to enter the store
3. Persuade them to buy

The aim of this book is to show retailers how to apply these principles to this store design.

You will learn:

- Store design psychology – what you must know to succeed
- Store design – Image selling
- How to use store design to increase sales
- Store design for increased customer flow
- Choosing your store colour and layout
- The best retail store lighting system
- How to wow customers with creative storefront design
- How to choose the right materials for store design
- Designing store for profit – design security
- Store design technologies

How to Market and Manage A Professional Firm Series: How to make 7 Figure annually as a doctor, dentist, accountant, lawyer, consultant and private security firm owner.

There are four elements essential for the success of any business:

1. Visionary leadership
2. Great people
3. Good system
4. Good marketing system

In the How to Market and Manage A Professional Firm Series, we teach professional entrepreneurs how to effectively utilize these four elements for the development of their businesses.

Many professionals are good technicians. They are good at their professions, however, when it comes to running business they are challenged.

The aim of the 7 Figure Code Books Series is to show professionals how to enhance their technical skills and apply similar levels of structural thinking into building a 7 Figure business.

There is no reason why a doctor or lawyer should not be able to easily make 7 Figure per annum. We show them how to achieve this in the How to Market and Manage A Professional Firm Series.

You will learn:

- How to create an effective business system that runs on auto-pilot
- How to recruit and retain only top talents
- How to develop an effective marketing system
- How to create new market for a product or service
- How the attract new clients and retain existing ones

Book Romeo

Book Romeo now by calling:
+44(0)78 650 49508
Or email: romeo@theprofitexperts.co.uk

www.ingramcontent.com/pod-product-compliance
Lightning Source LLC
Chambersburg PA
CBHW071357170526
45165CB00001B/79